Crescent Color Guide to Classic CARS

Crescent Color Guide to

Classic
CARS

Peter Roberts

Crescent Books
New York

First English edition published by
The Hamlyn Publishing Group Limited
London · New York · Sydney · Toronto
Astronaut House, Feltham, Middlesex, England

Library of Congress Catalog Card Number: 80-65953
ISBN 0-517-31852-0

This edition is published by Crescent Books,
a division of Crown Publishers, Inc.
a b c d e f g h

Phototypeset by Tradespools Limited, Frome, Somerset
Printed by Litografía A. Romero, S. A.
Santa Cruz de Tenerife, Canary Islands (Spain)
D. L. TF. 350 – 1980

*The publishers and author would like to express their gratitude to the following organizations
and persons for their help in research and for supplying photographs for this book, and for
valuable editorial assistance.*

Adam Opel AG., Russelsheim am Main; Alfa Romeo SpA, Milan; Aston Martin Lagonda (1975) Ltd.;
Automobiles Citröen, Paris; Automobiles Peugeot SA, Paris; Mr. Michael Banfield; Mr. Cecil Bendall;
British Leyland UK Ltd.; M. Phillipe Charbonneaux; Chrysler Corporation, Detroit; Citröen Cars Ltd.;
Daimler-Benz AG., Stuttgart; Fiat Motor Company (UK) Ltd.; Ford Motor Company Ltd. and Mrs.
Sheila Knapman; Ford US of Dearborn; General Motors Ltd.; Lips Autotron at Drunen, Holland; Lotus
Group of Companies; Maranello Concessionaires Ltd.; Mercedes-Benz (United Kingdom) Ltd.; Mrs
Karin Mitra; Musée de l'Automobile Française; Panther Westwinds Ltd.; Porsche Cars Great Britain
Ltd.; Régie Nationale des Usines Renault, France; Renault Ltd.; Rolls-Royce Motors Ltd.; The
Shuttleworth Collection; Vauxhall Motors Ltd.

Thanks also to Mr. Michael Worthington-Williams of Sotheby's for his able help in
matters editorial and research.

Photographic acknowledgments
Neill Bruce: pages 43 top, 48 top, 51 top, 60, 66 top, 71 bottom right, 76. Nicky Wright: pages 53,
55, 56 right, 59 bottom, 64 top, 64 bottom, 72 top. (Photographs on front cover and pages 55, 56 right
and 59 bottom are also by permission of the Auburn-Cord-Duesenberg Museum).
All other photographs are from the Peter Roberts Collection.

Front cover:	1931 Duesenberg J (Nicky Wright)
Back cover:	Porsche Turbo (Maurice Rowe)
Endpapers:	Lamborghini Countach (Maurice Rowe)
Title spread:	1923 Alvis Ducksback (Neill Bruce)
Contents spread:	Mercedes-Benz 7·1-litre SSK (Peter Roberts Collection)

Contents

The Dawn of the
Automobile Age (1885-1904) 6

Sporting Challenge 21

The Golden Years 34

The Years Between
the Wars 47

The New Generation
(1950-1980) 61

The Dawn of the Automobile Age (1885-1904)

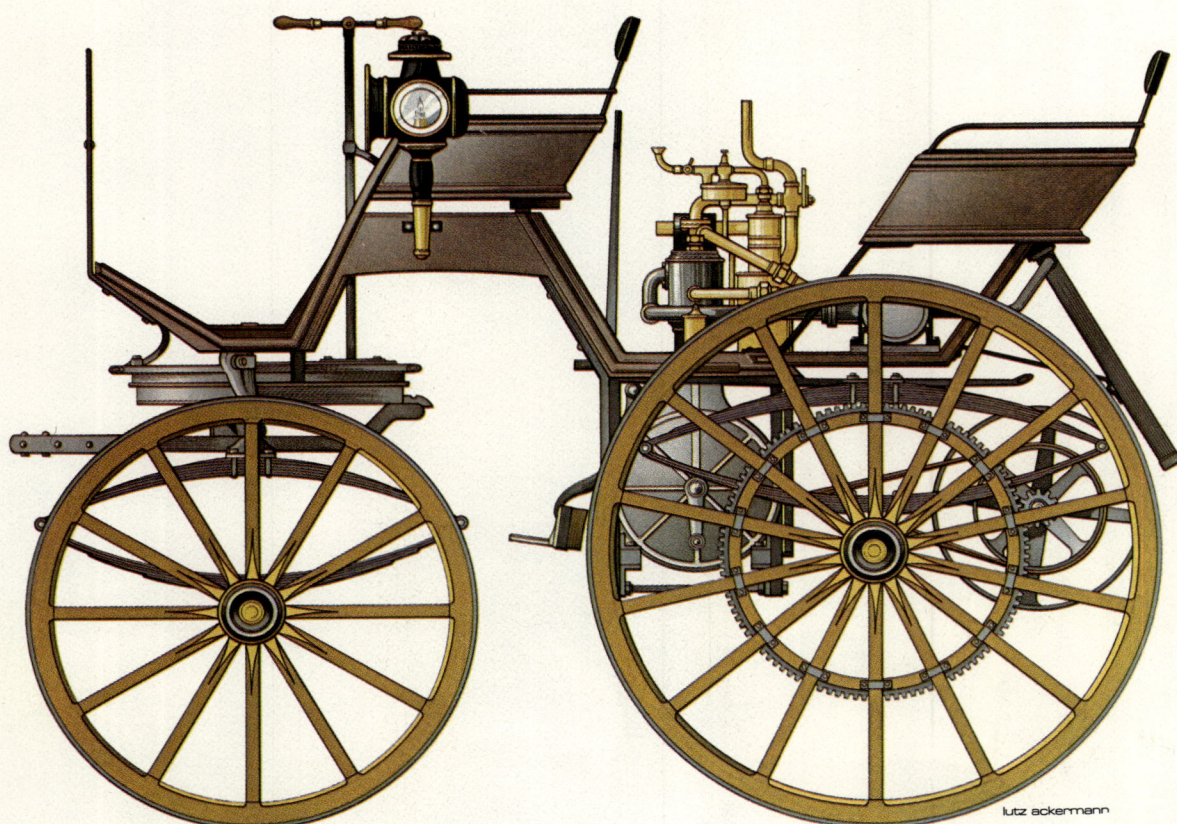

This light carriage, fitted with a single cylinder engine in 1886, was Daimler's first true automobile. Later he installed his engine in a river launch and an airship.

The scene is a small town in Germany, the time New Year's Eve, a century ago, in the small dining-room of a modest suburban house. Outside in the yard is a small workshop. The year 1880 is just ten minutes away.

The pretty young housewife turns to her 35-year-old engineer husband: 'Karl, let's go over to the workshop and try our luck once more. Something tells me that we should try one last time.'

Bertha and Karl Benz walk over to the little engine he had been building over the past weeks. Benz seizes the cranking handle, turns it, his heart pounding. . .

This is what Karl Benz, father of the first practicable automobile, said years later of the next historic moments. 'The engine started to go put-put-put and the music of the future sounded with regular rhythm. We both listened to it for a full hour, never tiring of the single note of its song. The two-cycle engine performed as no magic flute in the world ever had. . .for we knew the greatest kind of happiness that evening in our poor workshop. Suddenly the bells began to ring out, ringing in an era which was to take on a new heartbeat from the use of this engine.'

Six years later Benz's first automobile had been built and tested in his backyard shop, using an improved version of the crude power unit that had been born on that New Year's Eve.

The first Benz 'Patent Motor Car' was considerably indebted to the cycle industry that was flourishing during that period. Cycle-type tubing

6

was used for the frame, cycle-type spoked wheels were used and chains and linkages of cycle design were employed in the Benz lightweight three-wheeler. The tiny ⅔ hp engine was a miracle of invention and innovation; its single cylinder had a slide inlet valve something like today's two-stroke unit, cooling was by water evaporation in a jacket round the cylinder. Karl Benz developed an ignition system which used coil, sparkplug and battery. The drive to the road wheels was by pulley and belt to a transmission shaft which had a differential, and by moving the belt from idler to working pulley the drive could be engaged and disengaged. Engine speed was controlled by changing the quantity of air admitted to the mixture of air/petrol vapour from a surface-type carburettor. Simple and rough were these systems, but how curiously modern those technical terms still sound to us a hundred years later.

Meanwhile, down at Cannstatt, a few miles away from the Benz home in Mannheim, another engineer was busy in his workshop. Gottlieb Daimler, 51 years old, had been working on a petrol engine for some time, and had made a compact, water-cooled, four-stroke, single-cylinder unit which he patented on 3 April 1885. Daimler's objective was to design an engine that could power any type of vehicle (unlike the Benz engine, which was designed specifically to propel a road carriage), and his first choice of experimental test-bed transport was a hobby-horse type motorcycle. He fitted it with his ½ hp motor, and trundled around his garden in the unwieldy 'single-track' machine. His loyal assistant and lifelong friend Wilhelm Maybach is credited with building this unit, one small enough to fit into the cramped space between the wheels of the cycle.

Daimler's second attempt at self-propelled road transport was more ambitious. He ordered an open family coach to be delivered to his premises, keeping his real intentions secret by saying that he wanted to give his wife a surprise birthday gift. Clandestinely he fitted a 1·1-hp engine into the rear floor-space of the carriage.

This unit was fired by hot tube ignition, a simpler method than that used by Benz but one which was less positive in action. The engine was mounted on rubber shock absorbers, the water fan-cooled (at first) and the gas-air mix preheated by exhaust gas – all pointers to the future and all on the world's joint-first automobile.

Daimler, visionary and pragmatist, fitted his engine into a river launch, running it up and down the local waterway, the Neckar, to everyone's astonishment. Then in 1887 he installed one in a streetcar, and later fitted out an airship which had been experimenting with steam engines, with a propeller-driving gas unit which took the dirigible on a successful first flight of 4 km (2½ miles).

Thus the first internal combustion engine-powered air and marine craft were launched, and the first shaky automobiles rattled over the cobbled roads of Germany – the ancestors, for good or ill, of today's teeming millions of vehicles.

Progress was slow at first, but by 1888 Benz had published his first advertisement, and the first sales had taken place. When Benz overcame the tricky technical problem of steering by the two front wheels (he had designed his first car as a three-wheeler to avoid the problems associated with two-wheel steering), had made his first four-wheeler, the Viktoria, and had moved on to the Velo, the world's first small standard production car, he moved into an early form of mass production. In 1894, the first year of the Velo, Benz sold 67 machines. The following year he sold 135; by 1900 annual sales had risen to 603. Then the result of a dramatic event in the automotive world hit the Benz sales graph.

In 1900 Daimler, who by this time was selling motor cars in several European countries as well as in the United States of America, had been engaged in motor sport for several seasons. That year his French agent Emil Jellinek, former racing driver and diplomat, had found the 23-hp Daimler from Canstatt far too unwieldy for hill-climbing competition. A driver had been killed conducting one of his cars up the La Turbie hill-climb contest near Monte Carlo. Jellinek persuaded the Daimler company (Gottlieb himself had died in 1900) to make a lower, longer model of increased horsepower.

Thus a new car entered the scene, and a new motor age opened. The 1901 Daimler product had so many advanced features that it rendered every other motor car obsolete overnight. With a beefy 35 hp from its 5·9-litre, four-cylinder engine fed by jet carburettors, the car scooped the field during the Spring meeting at Nice in March 1901, winning almost every prize offered in competition.

Emil Jellinek had promised to sell a first series of 36 of the new cars if they were made to his specifications. His order book was soon crammed with the addresses of would-be buyers.

One factor, apart from the obvious technical advances of the car, aided its universal sales success. There had been a certain amount of German sabre-rattling in Europe at the time, and Jellinek had insisted that the car be given a less Germanic name than Daimler. It was agreed that the 1901 model should be named after his 11-year-old daughter Mercédès. As French writer Paul Mayan, secretary general of the French Automobile Club was forced to admit in print after the debut of the new car at Nice, 'We are now in the era of the Mercedes', which must have been galling for a patriot whose allegiances would have been fiercely with the French Mors or the great Panhard et Levassor motor company which had hitherto been leading the automobile world in reputation.

FRANCE TAKES THE LEAD
The experimental age of pre-motoring development had been mainly in Germany. Marcus had made an early self-propelled cart driven by an internal combustion engine, Nikolaus Otto produced a four-stroke gas engine as early as 1876 in his Deutz factory (where the technical director has been the young Gottlieb Daimler) and the brilliant work of Benz and Daimler in the last years of the nineteenth century pointed to the continuance of German leadership in the field of road transport. However, the heartland of the motor industry had moved to France from Germany, the country of its nativity, during the 1890s when licences to make the engine were granted by Daimler to a number of French companies.

Perhaps the French had more commercial enterprise for they rapidly stole the scene from their neighbouring country during the years of automobile development at the fold of the centuries, forming automobile

Above: The Mercedes, a car named after the daughter of Daimler's French agent, appeared in 1901 and rendered all other motor vehicles obsolete overnight. This is the 1902 Mercedes-Simplex tourer, its direct successor.

Above right: The Stahlradwagen or 'wire-wheeler' car of 1889 was fitted with a twin-cylinder engine, and was Daimler's first vehicle to break away from carriage-building tradition.

Right: The bizarre Schlumpf collection of antique cars in Mulhouse, France, was discovered after many years of being kept secret by its owners. This is a nineteenth century steam vehicle that as yet has defied identification.

associations, mounting sporting contests, creating speed records, forging new companies, marketing new vehicles. So enthusiastic were both manufacturers and buyers in France during those formative motoring years that the 'official' language of motoring and motor sport is still French.

Certainly the 1889 Paris Universal Exposition had created a French interest in mechanical power. Daimler was there with his new 'Steel Wheeler' and some of his engines. The spindly car, built on cycle lines, was not of great interest to the crowds packing the exhibition, but the uses to which his engine could be put caught the imagination of several people, including a lady and her constant companion, a Monsieur Emile Levassor. The lady's husband had recently died and his last advice had been that she foster their current business relationship with Herr Daimler – he had been a representative of Daimler's company – and that she take over his recently agreed rights to make the latest Daimler engine under licence in France.

Mme. Sarazin's companion Levassor married her, and by 1890, with his partner René Panhard, had made and sold the first of the engines. Panhard and Levassor had given permission to Armand Peugeot to install the engine in a carriage, although in fact they produced their first automobile slightly earlier than Peugeot's 1891 quadricycle.

History has more to say about the first Panhard than of the Peugeot. The original Panhard had its engine midships, under the seats. But for several reasons the unit was moved to the front of the car (the official explanation was that the steering system would be more stable; an unofficial one was that the ladies found the seats too hot) thus

9

unconsciously setting down the conventional layout of today's motor cars – front engine, followed by clutch, gearbox and drive to the road wheels. Its gearbox was exposed to the elements and gave a choice of indirect ratios, bevel drive to a cross-shaft and side chains, a design that became known as the *Systeme Panhard*. It was based on Levassor's experience of lathe-belt speed-change systems, and as he said: '*C'est brusque et brutal, mais ça marche!*' – 'It's rough and brutal, but it works!'

The Peugeot company had long been in the business of making metal parts for anything from crinolines to bicycles. Armand, scion of the ancient family, had been studying engineering in England and had foreseen the future of motor transport. His first motor carriage employed the Daimler V-twin power unit at the rear with its water cooled through the tubular, cycle-type frame on which the car was built. The steering was by cycle-type handlebar.

A Peugeot 4-place *vis-a-vis* (passengers and driver sit face-to-face) made the first-ever long-distance, cross-country run in 1891 when it was driven 2,047 km (1,272 miles) following the Paris-Brest-Paris cycle race 'without a moment's trouble' at a speed of around 15 km/h (9 mph). Peugeot, with their cycle-designing experience, seemed to be able to produce more reliable vehicles than the heavier, more cumbersome Panhards of the late Nineties, and the cars had markedly better driving characteristics, partly due to their superior suspension.

During the early twentieth century large numbers of small manufacturers mushroomed (the total number of U.S. manufacturers from

A Panhard-Levassor of about 1895, with twin-cylinder engine. By this time the *Systeme Panhard* was being copied by many other manufacturers.

De Dion-Bouton, circa 1899; a famous advertisement showing a Model D voiturette, two tricycles, a quadricycle and a De Dion steam bus.

pioneering days to the present stands at well over 2,000). Many were merely backyard tinkerers who soon sank without trace, but some, with perhaps a past history of engineering in cycles, sewing machines or other light machinery, began to flourish, including those whose background had been electrical and who were pushing ahead with battery-powered transport, or those in the locomotive field who favoured steam as the motive power for road vehicles.

De Dion-Bouton was one of the most popular French makes of the time. Born of an alliance between nobleman Comte de Dion and steam engineer Georges Bouton, the company first made steam vehicles – *automobiles à vapeur* – but changed to petrol in 1883. De Dion tricycles and voiturettes (light cars) using a high-speed engine of unusual efficiency were more numerous than any other marque at the turn of the century, and European city streets rang to the warning bells of the little French 'Ding-Dongs'.

France was making a bewildering variety of automobiles by the time Edward, Prince of Wales reached the English throne, from the little Decauville to the massive Mors and De Dietrich racers. Darracq, Delaunay-Belleville, Gobron-Brillie were representatives of the more aristocratic products, while dozens of cheaper cars were made in high hopes of mass sales.

Henry Ford had made his first internal combustion engine back in 1893. His first car, powered by the unit seen here, could reach a top speed of 25 mph.

Formal dress in a De Dion-Bouton! This one is an 1899 voiturette with a water-cooled unit mounted at the rear, and two-speed transmission.

The name of Louis Renault appears early in this field. At 21 this young son of a middle-class French family living at Billancourt in suburban Paris was annoying the neighbours by working at all hours in the shed at the bottom of the garden. Firstly adapting a De Dion tricycle, then building a four-wheeler of his own in 1899, he persuaded a few friends to order his new product. Within a year the three brothers, Louis, Marcel and Fernand, had formed a company. Six months later they had sold 60 vehicles and had made the world's first saloon car. Louis Renault was acknowledged France's first captain of industry by the time he was 29 and was made a Chevalier de la Legion d'Honneur in 1906. His company was turning out over 10,000 cars a year by 1914 and had opened branches all over the world.

AMERICAN PROGRESS
In the U.S.A. the automotive industry at the turn of the century still had its feet firmly stuck in the muddy waters of fundamental automotive problems, such as making a choice between steam, electric or gasoline power, and in the equally sticky mud of its appalling road system. The general opinion of American roads of that time led most international travellers to opine that it was easier to go around the North American landmass than over it.

However, although U.S. pioneers lagged far behind the technical standards of French and German manufacturers, suffering from lack of knowledge of what was being developed in Europe, they plunged into this new industry with typical American application and energy.

The brothers Duryea had built a Benz-based machine, successfully tested it, and had even raced it by 1895. Electric vehicles had been built and sold, but their range was restricted to city limits by their need for regular battery charging. Steam vehicles had been tried a generation earlier, and still had a large following. Hiram Maxim had offered his internal-combustion-engined lightweight car to a Colonel Albert Pope, who turned it down as 'people wouldn't want to sit on top of an explosion'. Colonel Pope started making electric cars with considerable success, a success that ironically led him eventually into the gas-engined field – to build a veritable empire of early vehicles.

But like the British motor industry, which was held back in pioneer days by diehard opinion and legislation, American automobile manufacturing was slowed down by an historic legal hiccup. In 1895 lawyer George Selden had cornered the patent on nearly every part of the early automobile, and for 16 years, until Henry Ford upset his patents claim in a lawsuit that became part of history, Selden played cat among the pigeons in the infant American industry, demanding that new auto makers pay up or cease business.

Farmer's boy Henry Ford had been in business for some time by 1911, the time of the great lawsuit, and had built his first engine back in 1893 out of gas-piping and wire. His first car, a lightweight quadricycle owing much to bicycle and soapbox ancestry, appeared three years later and was remarkable in that its two tiny cylinders could take it along at up to 25 mph although it had several small disadvantages such as no brakes or reverse gear!

By the turn of the century, every American with the remotest claim to manufacture had plunged, it seemed, into the industry.

The Stanley brothers, who produced the classic steam car, were formerly photographic plate makers; George Pierce, later to produce the acclaimed Pierce-Arrow, had made birdcages and bicycles, young Ransom Olds was a bookkeeper at his father's repair works, James Packard had manufactured electric cables, and David Buick was a plumber. Many of the early twentieth-century auto makers of America, quality companies and monkeywrench engineers alike, went to the wall before many years had passed (and many more vanished during the Depression of 1929), but some went on to found marques that would become household names of the period – makes like Packard, Marmon, Cadillac, Buick, Stutz, Locomobile, and so many others.

Many made light, high-wheeled autos, ranch or farm buggies that became the classic form of American car in a period when the roads were

still deep in mire. One such was the Holsman, a two-cylinder lightweight with an ability to negotiate rough tracks and to ford shallow rivers. This model sold in considerable numbers in the Mid-west where it suited road conditions admirably.

But the most popular American car in the buggy tradition was the little Curved Dash Olds. Produced by Ransom Eli Olds in Lancing, Michigan, the 'Merry Olds' was a classic in many ways at the time of its introduction, and has certainly become a sought-after classic today.

The Curved Dash brought motoring to many who would not have been able to afford a more luxurious vehicle. Simplicity was the keynote of the car, and Olds brought the first rudiments of quantity production to its manufacture. He also introduced mass-marketing techniques for a low-price car, giving confidence to investors who had earlier considered the auto industry a somewhat hare-brained gamble. The Olds works also proved to be a training ground for many budding engineers who were to move on to their own auto-making businesses. The Curved Dash, with its tiller steering and single-cylinder unit giving 'one chug per telegraph pole' and 7 hp, rolled into the history books by rapidly topping the sales charts (425 in 1901, 5508 in 1904) and by performing a number of marathon coast-to-coast trips watched by an admiring American public.

A car that came to be called the 'Standard of the World' was the modestly-launched Cadillac. In 1903 Henry Leland, who had been associated with Ford's early ventures, took over the car-making side of the company that Henry had left, renaming the product Cadillac. It had a

13

similar overall design to Ford's Model A, the first car to be produced by his new Ford Motor Company, but under Leland's meticulous control soon became known for its superb engineering quality. At a time when every automobile was built individually with parts machined and trimmed to match only a single-partner unit, Leland's insistence on the accuracy of each part of the vehicle in manufacturing allowed an astonishing demonstration of precision when three similar Cadillacs were completely dismantled, the parts scrambled and reassembled, and the cars immediately driven.

A turn in the Bois for madame in her Peugeot Victoria, circa 1892. It was powered by a 1282-cc engine built under Daimler licence.

Ford No 1, completed in June 1896 and powered by a twin-cylinder, chain-driven engine which was surprisingly reliable.

BRITAIN ON THE ROAD

Britain, until 1896 still under the restrictive laws which stated that motor vehicles should not exceed 4 mph, was also, like America, lagging behind the European motor world. French and German enthusiasts were enjoying the new sport of motor racing whilst in Britain it was still necessary for a footman to precede the vehicle. Numbers of influential 'autocarists' were lobbying in high places, however. The Prince of Wales had been out for a spin in a new British Daimler and had caught motoring fever. Others in Parliament were persuaded to the cause. But most authority was still firmly in the horse era, and both the police and the courts were heavily biased against the motorist. One sometimes cannot help agreeing with some of the diehards though, for early automobiles and their drivers were often very real dangers to children and animals, and were certainly polluters of the countryside and urban regions with their great plumes of following dust.

The country had its share of forward-looking engineers, however, men who had seen developments in Germany and in France and were moving

Durkopp of Germany made this little Panhard-based two-cylinder 8-hp vehicle in 1901. They sold as Watsonias in Britain, and under the name of Canello-Durkopp in France.

Below: First Fiat. This poster of Fiat's initial product was seen in 1899. The 3½ hp model was soon succeeded by front-engined models.

Bottom: Mass production pioneer. The Curved Dash Oldsmobile was the first quantity-built automobile in the U.S.A. This is a 1901 model.

towards motor manufacture as fast as they could. F. W. Lanchester, a Midlands engineer, made his first prototype in 1895, a car that, like that of Karl Benz, he had built from the ground up without reference to traditional carriage construction. The result was a vehicle with a centrally mounted, horizontally-opposed, twin-cylinder, air-cooled engine which had an unusually smooth and quiet operation. His early cars, and later Lanchesters, were always unorthodox and advanced for their time, and whilst the company finally failed, it made numbers of important pioneering steps in automotive engineering.

Several small companies had begun to copy Continental models before 1900, but one of the earliest serious entrants into the field was Herbert Austin, a young man engaged in the somewhat seasonal work of managing the Wolseley Sheep Shearing Machine Company. To fill in he began making two light three-wheeler vehicles based on the Léon Bollée he had seen on a business trip to France.

Austin's work for Wolseley resulted in the first four-wheeled model being offered to the British public in 1899, and Royalty, in the person of Queen Alexandra, purchased a Wolseley in 1903.

Austin himself however had a disagreement with his directors about design – he wanted to produce engines with horizontal cylinders while his company wished to build vertical engines – which led him to set up his own company in 1906, the Austin Motor Company at Longbridge near Birmingham in the industrial Midlands of England.

The Daimler Motor Syndicate had been formed as far back as 1893 at Coventry under Gottlieb Daimler's patent. It produced its first cars in 1896 under the banner of entrepreneur H. J. Lawson who, like Selden in America, had attempted (eventually unsuccessfully) to corner the automotive market in Great Britain.

The turn of the century saw the first glimmer of an emerging industry, rather than an unrelated number of engineering projects. Napier, well known as printing machinery makers, had brought out their first series model, based on Panhard-Levassor design; American Wilbur Gun from Springfield, Ohio had started building small tri-cars in England, reliable little vehicles that evolved into the Lagonda sports cars that captured a large *aficionado* market in later years. Another marque born then was Sunbeam, product of the firm of John Marsden, the tinplate and japanning company.

The marine engineering company, Vauxhall Ironworks Ltd., on the banks of the Thames in west London, was also casting about for other

work, and entered the automotive field, one of the few pioneering companies in Britain still producing today a car bearing its original name. The same year as the Vauxhall made its debut another small company, which had been in the steam truck business for a time, decided that the fashion in transport was changing rapidly and produced the first Thornycroft internal combustion engined car, later models of which showed distinct similarities to the early Mercedes as did a high proportion of larger cars made during the first five years of the twentieth century.

Engineer Henry Royce had driven his first motor car out of his workyard in Manchester in April 1904 and had offered the Press a spin. All who where privileged to ride in the little 1·8-litre two-cylinder, shaft-driven Royce eulogized about its silence and smooth operation, and as one scribe wrote: 'The Royce car made all others sound like an avalanche of tea-trays!' When later in 1904 Royce met the Hon. Charles Rolls who had been selling French cars in London, the scene was set for the birth of the 'Best Car in the World', as the world called the Rolls-Royce.

By 1904–5, the end of the truly pioneering era, much of Europe was deeply involved in the motor industry. Germany had established a high reputation with Benz and Daimler, still separate companies, making advanced four-cylinder cars (the first six-cylinder Daimler, the Mercedes tourer, appeared in 1906). Opel, formed as a sewing machine and cycle company, had broken into the field, first with an alliance with the French Darracq company then in 1902 making their own complete cars in the family works in Rüsselsheim near Frankfurt am Main. Opel's first home product, a tidy little 10-hp with a two-cylinder 1884-cc power unit, was to set them on the road that took them into the lead as German motor manufacturers before the disastrous Depression of the early 1930s.

ITALY'S EMPIRE
South of the Alps, Italy, largely unsung as one of the real pioneers of road transport, started relatively late in the motor field. One of the oldest and most respected marques, Isotta-Fraschini, dates from 1899 (and continued for exactly half a century, during which time the car acquired an almost legendary reputation for sportive luxury), and other Italian classics – Lancia, Alfa Romeo, Maserati, Ferrari, Lamborghini – appeared on the scene considerably later.

The Italian scene is, and always has been, dominated by the giant Fiat concern in Turin. Fiat – *Fabbrica Italiana di Automobili Torino* – was one

Ideally suited to early U.S. Middle West roads, this high-wheeled Holsman Rambler of 1902 was made in Chicago. Its simple twin-cylinder unit and spartan construction enabled it to be sold cheaply in the U.S.A.

Above: 'The Standard of the World' was the claim of the Cadillac Motor Car Co. of Detroit. This 1906 10 hp Model K two-seater could be transformed into a four-place tourer.

Left: Lanchester 1903, 12 hp and extremely unorthodox with its centrally-mounted engine and side-tiller steering.

man's dream, backed by a syndicate of wealthy Turin financiers. Giovanni Agnelli had been a junior officer in the Italian cavalry, had left the army, persuaded some local bankers to buy an old cycle works and there made his first automobile in 1899.

Agnelli's small car, a mite old-fashioned for the day with its flat-twin rear engine, face-to-face seating and huge Victoria canopy, sold 20 examples, a healthy start for the infant company. Fiat fortunes increased with the speed of a runaway horse. By 1903 the company was producing trucks as well as several car models. Two years later Fiat was in ship-building and ball-bearings, and was the country's leading manufacturer of marine engines. Aircraft and locomotives completed the company's coverage of the transport world. Today Fiat is one of the largest and most powerful manufacturers *of any type* in the world.

Always well advanced in engineering and manufacturing technology, the motor makers of Italy have continuously produced cars that have qualified for the accolade of classic, confirming the old saw that 'Every Italian is an engineer and every engineer an artist'.

Opel-Darracq 1902. This year the German company imported Darracq chassis, mounting their own bodies on the cars. Single cylinder; top speed 45 km/h.

Three years into the new century saw dramatic developments in the motor industry – and in the motoring habit. The years of experimentation were not over, yet much of car design had become established. By 1903–4 most well-constructed cars were using the *Systeme Panhard* with the engine settled down in front of the car and the drive train through clutch and box and chains or shaft to a differential and rear road wheels.

Motoring was still, in Europe at least, a hobby for the rich, something 'to indulge in between fishing and ping-pong' as one contemporary journal put it, and a drive into the country was an accepted weekend

pastime – as long as it didn't interfere with hunting.

Only in America was the new transportation taken seriously by the public, and here the buyers were, more often than not, doctors or travelling salesmen whose gratitude to the motor industry was unbounded after years in the saddle or on a bouncing buckboard.

Most cars were still open to the elements. Designers were still so occupied with getting the car to its destination that weather protection was virtually ignored, except for the type of clothes recommended for travelling. But although the man-in-the-street (even in the streets of London or New York) would be quite likely to traverse town without seeing a single car, automobile development was moving forward rapidly and irreversibly.

In 1903 world production of cars was 61,927, a fantastic number for an industry only a bare ten years old, and considering that the horse was still king of the road in the minds of a vast majority of the world's population. France still led the field commercially, producing some 30,000 cars that year, a figure that indicated that she was expanding eagerly into the new age. Technically, the 1901 Mercedes had given manufacturers a jolt, one that soon became a shot-in-the-arm as engineers buckled down to the task of copying and improving on the advanced German machinery.

Complete cars were not yet made and sold as single items. The chassis was purchased, then the form of body discussed with the coachmakers, built carefully and laboriously by hand, and fitted on to the frame. Naturally most of the bodybuilders came directly from the horse-drawn coachbuilding trade, with the result that car shapes, although long past the horseless carriage stage, were often still adorned with the weighty curlicues and decorations of an earlier era. Only the smaller, cheaper vehicles seemed to escape the rather stultifying tradition; with their construction designed for economy and lightness there was little room for décor or Victorian comfort.

Some five years into the new century the aim of motor engineers had changed subtly. One of Europe's foremost writers on the subject has put it more clearly than most. Said Laurence Pomeroy Jnr: 'From 1885 to 1895 men struggled to make the car go. From 1896 to 1905 they contrived to make it go properly. Between 1907 and 1915 they succeeded in making it go beautifully.'

Former steam-lorry makers Thornycroft produced their first car in 1903. This is a late model of that year, with finned tube radiator.

Vauxhall Ironworks Ltd. moved from river craft to cars in 1903. This is their first offering to the public – a 6 hp runabout.

Sporting Challenge

Competition is natural to man. Rapid travel has always been one of his fondest ambitions. The search for personal transport has been another. And when in the course of history science offered the chance for him to compete in a new form of mechanical transport, his enthusiasm knew few bounds.

The first competitive motoring events were designed as endurance tests. Autocars, as many people called them, were wildly unreliable during the formative years of the 1890s, and most early vehicles were not used as serious transport to a destination but were leisure objects, used at weekends by the wealthy for their amusement.

However, by 1894 one man at least, the *chef des informations* of a French magazine *Le Petit Journal* decided to encourage designers and owners by mounting the world's first motor sporting contest, a reliability trial.

From Paris to Rouen was a distance of some 120 rural kilometres (75 miles) and on the morning of 22 July some 21 vehicles, from cumbersome iron-clad steam trucks to light-weight phaetons on their cycle-type chassis and wheels, set off from the Porte Maillot in Paris for the waiting crowds at the ancient cathedral city of Rouen.

Although the winner would be the vehicle that, as the regulations stated, was 'without danger, easily handled by its driver, and of low running costs', the spirit of speed competition was evident before the first batch had left the cobbles of the Porte Maillot. Finally a Panhard and a Peugeot, both using the Daimler V-twin engine, were awarded joint first prizes. The long, nerve-shredding, heart-pounding story of motor racing had begun, with its colour and its victories and tragedies.

Nothing could stop that coterie of sportive Frenchmen from mounting another event the following year. . .and a dozen more races in the

Peugeot 1895. This model was similar to the one that took part in motor sport's first event, from Paris to Rouen in 1894.

next. . .until national borders had been crossed in the name of motor sport, and Germany and Italy and America had joined in, and finally Britain had found a vehicle worthy of competing with the world's best – the Mors, Mercedes, Panhard, Darracq and De Dietrich cars.

By 1902 capital-to-capital races were the vogue, long-distance marathons that would include dizzy mountain ranges and fast straight sections where speeds were already topping 140 km/h (90 mph).

The great race that year was from Paris to Vienna, with another race running concurrently over the same route, from Paris to Innsbruck in

Austria. The longer race of 1,120 km (695 miles) was won by a small Renault car competing in the voiturette class, driven by Marcel Renault against vastly more powerful opposition that included the much-vaunted Mercedes – the car everyone thought should win easily. The Paris-to-Innsbruck race for the Gordon Bennett Trophy, a cup donated by the American newspaper editor of that name and run at the same time, was won by Englishman Selwyn F. Edge in a lightweight 6·5-litre Napier, the first time Napier or any other British car had won an international sporting event.

By this time publicity created by a win in an important race brought customers to the maker of the victorious car, a fact that did not escape the notice of manufacturers who were now putting great energy into producing sporting vehicles – not necessarily for sale to the public – and training racing drivers to handle them.

Racing on public roads soon became too dangerous to be allowed to continue following a number of accidents, particularly in the Paris-Madrid race of 1903. By 1906 speed competitions had been confined to closed roads which could form a continuous circuit.

The first major event to be held under these conditions was at Le Mans in the Sarthe region of France, a race which was the first of today's annual Grand Prix series.

The 103-kilometre (64-mile) circuit was over closed public roads, joined into a rough triangle by a temporary connecting road. The weather was intolerably hot. Earlier, dust had plumed up over the circuit at the slightest breeze. To lay this hazard the *piste* was tarred, later causing an even worse hazard as melting tar sprayed up into the faces of the drivers.

There was a large entry. Thirty-seven teams had brought their cars from all the European manufacturing countries except Britain, who could

De Dietrich entered this chain-driven two-seater car in the Paris Madrid race of 1903. At this time the French car was beginning to make its mark in motorsport.

22

This Renault was the surprise winner of the Paris-Vienna race of 1902, with Marcel Renault at the wheel. The 3·7-litre car averaged 62 km/h (39 mph) over the 615-mile race.

not find a suitable vehicle. France put 28 cars on the start-line, amongst which was the Renault team.

The No. 1 driver for the Renault *équipe* was Hungarian Ferenc Szisz; his car a 13-litre (not by any means large for the day when compared with the 18·3-litre Panhards in the race) with shaft-drive, a feature of Renault cars from the earliest days, and one that was not then the accepted method of transmitting power to the road wheels, which were usually driven by heavy, rattling chains. The car also had another innovation – detachable wheel rims. With an expected half-a-dozen punctures during the long race, this quick-change system proved a distinct advantage when most other competitors had to cut off the old tyre, struggle with safety bolts to put on a new one, pump it up and restart the engine. The new rims reduced changing time by vital minutes.

Held under a brassy June sun, the 1906 Grand Prix de l'Automobile Club de France, as the French Grand Prix is still officially called, was a classic that went straight into the record books. Szisz won the long race at

Hispano-Suiza Alfonso 1912. Based on a race-winning voiturette of the same marque, this classically-engineered sports car was best known with a 3·6-litre engine.

a daunting average speed of 101 km/h (62·8 mph), pursued hotly by Nazzaro's 100-hp Fiat, after a two-day drive of almost 13 hours.

The following year the French Grand Prix was run at Dieppe in Normandy, when fortunes were reversed. This was Fiat's great racing year. The first two cars past the flag at the French race in 1907 were of the same marques as the previous year but this time Nazzaro's Fiat led the Renault driven by the Hungarian Szisz. Fiat cars in this, their *annus mirabilis*, also won the other two major races that year, the event over the treacherous roads of Sicily organized by wealthy promoter Vincenzo Florio earlier in the year, and the Kaiserpreis, the race held for touring cars over the Taunus Mountains near Frankfurt in Germany. The little Italian driver Nazzaro, son of a coal merchant, won all three for Fiat, a treble victory that Fiat never surpassed. Twenty-six-year-old Nazzaro's win in the French event was in Fiat's most powerful car, the 16·3-litre, 130-hp, four-cylinder Corso designed by Carlo Cavalli, one-time lawyer turned technical director.

END OF THE MONSTERS
The demise of the multi-litre monsters of the first years of the century came shortly after it was seen that lighter cars with smaller, more efficient engines, could outpace the giants. Even Panhard, one of the founders of the dinosaur breed, began to bring their engines down a few litres, as designers realized that brute power and piston size availed little against efficient design. By 1914, the end of the Edwardian racing era, engines had become far smaller, the winner of the French Grand Prix of that year being a racing Mercedes of just 4·5 litres.

Meanwhile, on the public roads, cars had taken several directions in design. Luxury cars, plush with traditional coachwork leavened by marine influence – portholes, brass speaking-tubes, port and starboard signals were *de rigueur* – vied with spartan tourers and sporting vehicles.

Vauxhall's classic model, the Prince Henry of 1914, housed a 3969-cc four-cylinder unit of 25 hp.

Top right: Descendant of the Prince Henry, the 4·5-litre (later 4·2) Vauxhall 30/98 first made in 1913, was highly successful in competition during the Twenties, yet could safely take the family out for a spin.

Prince Heinrich of Prussia had offered a trophy in 1907 for a trial of cars that could be used on the road, and that could not in any way be termed racing cars. From the third of these events in 1910 emerged two vehicles that were perhaps the first true sports cars. One, an Austro-Daimler designed by Dr. Ferdinand Porsche, housed a 5·7-litre unit, old-fashioned but tough, and the other, a car that was closer to the standard touring car of the day, a 3-litre Vauxhall. The Vauxhall's reliability at the 1910 German trials had caught the eye of the public, and its designer, Laurence Pomeroy, had given it a 75 mph capability. Amateur racers at Britain's only motor racing circuit at Brooklands began to use this model

Above: Few cars are remembered with more affection than the Bentleys of the Twenties. This is a 1929 4398 cc (blown) Bentley at a vintage meeting in Britain.

Fiat 'Mephistopheles'
the huge 18·155 cc
racer that challenged
– and beat – a Napier
at Brooklands in
1908. It was rebuilt in
1922 and broke the
world speed record in
1924.

(now dubbed the Prince Henry Vauxhall) in stripped-down form, and several single-seaters were made. The Prince Henry created numbers of speed records and captured major rally trophies but could still be marketed as a car in which to take the family out for a Saturday spin.

Vauxhall's Prince Henry was succeeded by the 30/98 (nobody knows to this day why the car was so called) in 1913, but only half a dozen were made before production was halted by the First World War. However, within its single pre-war season the Vauxhall 30/98 had notched up an impressive score of victories in hill-climbing, racing and reliability trials – and this car too could be flexible and accommodating enough to be used with safety for ordinary motoring. The 30/98, Vauxhall's most illustrious car, was built in various forms until 1926, scoring 75 'firsts' between 1920 and 1923 in sporting events, and was certainly the finest fast tourer made in Britain in the Twenties, marred only by its somewhat feeble brakes. It is still acclaimed as one of the world's greatest all-round cars.

At the time of the Prince Henry's success another sportive model in the luxury class had become a byword in Europe. Swiss engineer Marc Birkigt made the first of his legendary Hispano-Suiza (Spanish-Swiss) cars in 1904 in Barcelona, Spain. His superbly engineered models, designed for the carriage trade, were popular in the royal household of Spain. The King, young Alfonso XIII, had two in his own motor stables.

In 1910 a smaller version of the marque won a light car race, and Birkigt based a production sports car on it. The Queen of Spain presented one to her husband that year, and the car became the Alfonso (Type 15T) model of the marque. Birkigt's new engine, one that was to prove significant throughout the automotive world, was enlarged to 3·6-litres, which gave 64 bhp at 2300 rpm. Birkigt's engine of 1912 (with ohc) was sold (history is a little vague about whether it was sold or pirated) to designer Ernest Henry who modified it into his four-cylinder, 16-valve, twin-overhead-camshaft unit that was to greatly advance engine efficiency and prove a watershed of racing engine design.

Both the design and the materials used in the Birkigt units played a vital part in aviation progress during the First World War, when the Swiss engineer designed and produced a light, water-cooled, V-8 engine that enabled French aircraft to outfly the Mercedes-powered German

aircraft during the earlier part of the war.

The world of motor sport was by now truly international. In America, permanent motor racing venues had long since brought the state of the sport up to European standards. Henry Ford had earlier made and broken world records in his extraordinary '999' racer, and Barney Oldfield had become a household name on both sides of the Atlantic with his exploits in the Blitzen Benz, when he took it at speeds of over 2 miles a minute in 1910. Indianapolis had been opened in 1909 and the first of the famous 500-mile races had taken place in 1911. Brooklands in England had opened two years earlier (1907), had seen several categories of racing, a 24-hour endurance demonstration with an average of 66 mph, had matched Britain's best – a Napier – against the might of the Fiat stable for a wager, and had become the heart of the sport in Britain.

THE TWENTIES AND THIRTIES

The First World War pushed technical knowledge forward rapidly. When the dust had settled, motor sport opened for business with the 1919 Targa Florio and the Indianapolis 500 where the Duesenberg straight-8 was seen in competition for the first time. For the next few years Duesenbergs and Millers were the doyens of the Indianapolis track, and from 1922 to 1936 no other marque won there.

On the road there were several choices for the young American sportsman. The low-slung, slow-revving 60-hp Stutz Bearcat, with its bucket seats, token windscreen, and little else in the way of comfort, alternated with its rival, the Mercer Type 35, as favourites with the sporting man-about-town even though they'd been around since before the war. Upmarket, Duesenberg was making cars that, apart from clocking numerous racing victories, were being eagerly sought by the new rich of America, the film fraternity. Duesenberg's Model J of 1923 and its later development, the supercharged 320-bhp Model SJ, had performances that can hardly be believed today, including a top speed of 129 mph.

In the sporting world of Europe perhaps three cars captured the imagination of the crowds above all others during the 1920s – the British Bentley, the French Bugatti, and the Alfa Romeo from Italy.

Bugatti, 2·3 supercharged Type 35B. More than 1,800 wins were scored during the 1920s by Type 35 Bugattis.

27

W. O. Bentley had shown his first car, a 3-litre, four-cylinder model in 1919, and sold his first in 1921, when it won its first race at Brooklands. A 3-litre Bentley won the notorious 1927 Le Mans after it had been all but wrecked with its two team cars at White House Corner.

The four-cylinder, 4398-cc Bentley, made from 1928 to 1931, was fitted with a supercharger by racing driver Sir Henry Birkin (doubling its output to 250 bhp) and is perhaps the most distinguished Bentley of all. It won the 1928 Twenty-four Hours of Le Mans and later raised the Brooklands record to 137·96 mph.

Milan-born Ettore Bugatti made his first car way back in 1901, and won a medal at the Milan exhibition that year. He moved to Alsace, then a part of Germany, and worked first for De Dietrich, then for Emil Mathis, and finally for Deutz in Cologne. There, in the cellar of his own house it is said, he built his own *Pur Sang*, his thoroughbred automobile, first of a line (less than a total of 10,000) of jewel-like cars that placed Bugatti amongst the automotive immortals. This car, the 1327-cc, four-cylinder Bugatti Type 13, was developed during 1908–9, and Ettore moved to Molsheim in Alsace to begin his own commercial production. The car was an immediate success. Bugatti, ever restless, also designed a tiny 2-seater, 850-cc car which he sold to Peugeot in 1912. It became the popular Peugeot Bébé.

Le Patron, as Bugatti was respectfully called, produced model after model and by 1924 had built what was to become his most famous car, the racing Type 35, first seen in 8-cylinder, in-line, 2-litre form, Bugatti's classic layout. During the following years the Type 35 was seen with

Left: *The* Classic Grand Prix car? The 250F Maserati built from 1954 to 1957 was not remarkably powerful yet could often beat the most formidable opposition. In 1957 it took Juan Fangio to World Championship in 2½-litre form.

Above: German domination of Grand Prix racing in the Thirties led to revived interest in 1½-litre voiturette events. The ERA seen here was a successful contender.

Left: The Alfa Romeo P2 introduced in 1924 was a highly successful 8-cylinder, 2-litre supercharged Grand Prix car designed by Vittorio Jano.

supercharger (everyone else was fitting one so Ettore reluctantly had to follow suit); as a 35A with a different engine and crankshaft; as a 1½-litre car; as a special 1100-cc racer for the 1962 Alsatian Grand Prix; as the 2.3-litre 35T modified for the Targa Florio. The Type 35B, an improved 35T, also had a 2.3-litre power unit, supercharged, and the 35C had a 2-litre supercharged engine. Bugatti conjured up a different car for each type of race over the years 1924–31. The engines were architecturally square and always (in his Type 35 racing versions) of eight cylinders. Bugatti juggled with his engines to considerable effect, for in the hectic seasons between 1924 and 1927 his cars won an astonishing total of 1,851 races.

The 'tween-years were the heyday of open cars which had pretensions to some sort of sporting performance. Britain led the open-air vogue – and produced some of the most practical motor cars. Names like MG, Alvis, Lagonda, Frazer-Nash, Aston Martin, contested sporting events – and often completed illegally on the public roads – with France's Amilcar, Salmson, BNC, Morel and other examples of the legion of up-and-coming French makers. In fact, over 300 firms in France were producing cars during the early Twenties, all but three of them long vanished. The survivors are Renault, Peugeot and Citroën, who wisely did not place all their energies or their faith in the production of sporting vehicles.

Italy, quietly building its motor industry, had by 1921 seen the prototype of Vincenzo Lancia's new concept of car design, dubbed the Lambda. By 1923 it was in full production, this advanced design with its narrow-angle, V-type, four-cylinder engine and near-monocoque construction (using the strength of its body's rigid frame instead of a heavy separate chassis), and independent front suspension. It was basically a fast tourer but various private owners entered their Lambdas in sporting events and many a Lambda driver carried off the main prizes. Alfa Romeo, the other Italian classic sporting marque, had opted for more active participation in Grand Prix motor racing, and by 1924, after Vittorio Jano had joined the company as designer, the 8-cylinder, 2-litre

Modern rallying. A French Alpine driven by Italian entrants roars up a steep road in the hills of central France during a recent Monte Carlo Rally.

P2 appeared in the grid – and won the first Grand Prix it entered.

From 1934 the Mercedes and Auto Union companies of Germany were building cars that would conform with regulations which stated that racing cars should not exceed 750 kilogrammes. This limitation also gave birth to the famous Alfa Romeo Monoposto which in the hands of little Tazio Nuvolari ('brakes are no good . . . they just make you go slower') defeated the powerful German opposition on its own home circuit, the Nurburgring, in 1935.

The rear-engined Auto Union, in spite of its awkward handling, took just two seasons to beat the world. In 1936 the car, with former motor cyclist Bernd Rosemeyer at the wheel, won six Grands Prix, proving that efficient design could get tremendous power out of an engine that complied with lightweight regulations designed primarily to prevent engines becoming too powerful.

Mercedes-Benz had also been encouraged by Hitler's government to show the world the calibre of its product, which it did by building for the 1934 season the first of the classic Silver Arrow racing cars, the straight-eight, 354-bhp W25. When this was followed in 1937 by the immensely powerful W125 (with a 5.7-litre engine giving 646 bhp) the Grand Prix racing world was effectively tied up by the Auto Union and Mercedes-Benz, hardly any other marque recording a win that season.

One effect of the German Grand Prix victories of the 1930s was to revive interest in 1½-litre voiturette racing in other European countries. Britain, particularly, eagerly entered this class of the sport and the Riley-based ERA (English Racing Automobiles Ltd.) began to figure in the winners' lists in competition with Maserati and Alfa Romeo.

Meanwhile Mercedes-Benz had in 1939, under the 3-litre Formula, brought out the W163, a V-12 car with double stage supercharging in which one compressor fed another, finally giving the engine a mind-boggling boost to 480 bhp. One can hardly imagine what sort of car would have come next from the incredible Stuttgart stable if war had not halted the sport.

MERCEDES RETURN TO THE GRID

After a 15-year break, Mercedes-Benz of Germany continued with very much the same programme as before. By 1954 the Silver Arrows Mercedes-Benz Grand Prix cars were on the grid contesting the supremacy of the Ferrari and Maserati *équipes*. After a try-out with some over-streamlined cars, the Mercs began to start leading the field again, and by the end of 1955 it was all over. The Mercedes-Benz W196, straight-8, 2·5-litre, 270-bhp cars had captured all the available silver-ware once more. The classic 250F Maserati, which had during the first half of the decade mopped up most of the prize money in the hands of Stirling Moss and Juan Fangio (who were now driving for Mercedes), and the Ferrari which had taken others of the world's best drivers to victory, were totally eclipsed by the Mercedes W196.

Above: The British-built Ford GT 40 (40 inches high) first challenged the supremacy of the Ferraris in the Le Mans 24 Hours in 1964. It won in 1966, 1967, 1968 and 1969.

Right: Current Formula 1 (Grand Prix) regulations restrict engine size to 3 litres or 1½ litres supercharged, and a minimum weight of 500 kilos. This is a Brabham-Alfa Romeo on a very wet Nurburgring.

Happily for Grand Prix racing, the Stuttgart company felt that in two seasons they had made their mark on the sport and on the public and could withdraw from the Formula 1 scene with honour, having proved in no uncertain fashion that Germany was back in the race in more ways than purely sporting terms.

Like most other sports, motor sport has grown rapidly in popularity during the past generation. Encouraged by sponsors – commercial organizations whose cash payments defray the costs of putting a car on the start-line in return for advertisement and publicity – the sport has diversified into a score of classes and categories in racing, record breaking, hill-climbing, rallying and various other mud-plugging branches of competition.

In Britain the sport received several shots in the arm after years in the doldrums trailing behind German and Italian contenders when in 1958 Mike Hawthorn of Britain became World Champion, albeit in an Italian Ferrari. Then when the world title went to drivers such as Jim Clark, John Surtees, Graham Hill and Jackie Stewart in cars such as the British-made Lotus and BRM, Britain became the centre of motor sport for some years.

Today the sport has again begun to move its focus to other regions, to France for instance where our imagination is captured by turbo-charged cars like the Renault, and back to Italy, to firms such as Alfa Romeo again producing a racing engine. But the majority of teams, most of whom use Ford engines for their cars, and all of whom bring new cars to the grid every year, modified to clip another fraction of a second off last year's lap times, are very much a result of British technological

supremacy – and the undoubted genius of one man, Colin Chapman, designer and builder of the Lotus.

Today many regions of the world are providing drivers from outside Europe. The 1978 World Champion, Mario Andretti is from the U.S.A., (the first American to win the championship since Phil Hill in 1961). In 1979 the world title was won by South African Jody Scheckter. Gilles Villeneuve is from Canada, Riccardo Patresse from Italy, Daly and Kennedy from Ireland and Zunino from Argentina, drivers from whom future world titles will almost certainly be drawn.

The Golden Years

During the period between the years of experiment (generally accepted to be from 1885 to 1905) and the great changes that the First World War brought in its wake, motoring enjoyed what was then considered to be, by motorists at least, a healthy proliferation, although in Britain the anti-automobile crusade was at its peak. There the unfortunate motorist risked a fine every time he left his private garage. The police and the courts filled the local coffers with the riches extracted from the intrepid motorist for exceeding 20 mph, or allowing a lamp to blow out – in days when roads were so free and empty that one may have met perhaps a dozen other motor vehicles on the 50-mile journey from London to Brighton.

However, new makes and models from every manufacturing country

Early kit car. A series of articles in a magazine of 1900 offered to show readers how to build a small car. The result – a tidy model (this is a 1904 example) with a two-cylinder, 8 hp engine.

Dutch aristocrat of 1904, now resident in the Lips Museum, Drunen, Holland. This dignified pot-bellied model has a four-cylinder engine of about 18 hp. The car appeared in the film *Genevieve*.

were pouring on to a still-hungry market during the middle of the first decade of the twentieth century, covering the entire range of size, sophistication, costs and purpose, from flimsy tricycles with mouse-power motors to large and solid products such as Belgium's classic Minerva, or the de Dietrich from Lunéville in Lorraine. Even kit cars were seen in magazines of the day, some, like the English Mechanic, born as a series of instructional articles, features that when the going got too hard for the reader (or the author) switched to advice on where to buy the requisite parts. The English Mechanic was in fact one of the better kits and several have weathered the fortunes of the past 80 years to delight us today.

By the middle of the Edwardian period every manufacturing country had its firmly-established top marques. France, a leading motoring nation, had the Delaunay-Belleville, round and dignified and ponderous, followed by several other worthies such as Mors, De Dietrich, and the twin originals, Panhard and Peugeot. The lesser breeds, Bollée, De Dion, Ader, Unic (of taxi fame) and Renault were beginning to produce models for the masses. Germany's Mercedes reigned supreme on the other side of the Rhine, with Opel climbing fast in production numbers. Benz, still over 20 years away from amalgamation with Daimler, was fighting back after the triumph of the market-capturing Mercedes, and was winning a number of sporting events, while the little cycle firm of NSU had presented its first modestly-powered cars.

The Cadillac had become the undisputed quality auto of America by 1906, hustled by a gaggle of companies aiming hard for the same customers, with the three Ps (Packard, Peerless and Pierce-Arrow) as chief rivals. . .and of course Henry Ford's Model T was at this time right there on the drawing board, almost ready to take over the world's transport problems.

There is one car that embodies all that was best of the Edwardian age, the *belle époque* of motoring, one model of one marque that more than any other epitomizes the craftsmanship, the rapidly advancing engineering techniques, the atmosphere and the philosophy of the era before the First World War – the Rolls-Royce Silver Ghost. Called by its purchasers, by its admirers, even by some of its competitors, the 'Best Car in the World' (it was never called so by its makers), the Rolls-Royce captured the imagination and the enthusiasm of the small, wealthy motoring public as no automotive product ever had before.

Even the story of the making of the first Rolls-Royce cars and the subsequent meeting of the two men who were to form the famous company is typical of the attitude of an age when British workmanship was so often best: Royce, the meticulous engineer who would not accept

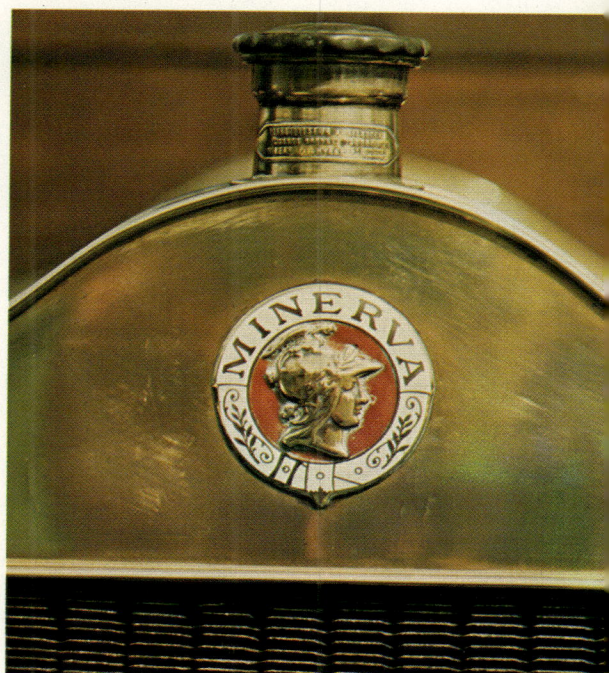

Another aristo, the Minerva, from Belgium. The 1909 model shown here was one of the first of the marque to use the Knight Sleeve valve engine, a silent and smooth unit used by several top makes.

anything less than perfection, and Rolls, whose agency for French cars left him unsatisfied with the quality of the product he was selling to the British public.

The first Royce car had been seen as early as 1904, an adaptation of a French Decauville that Henry Royce had brought over to his Manchester workshop, a 10-hp, two-cylinder machine with overhead inlet valves. The Hon. Charles Rolls heard of it – the only British car that could match and even improve on the continental makes – met the dour Royce, drafted an agreement, and formed the company that was to become the doyen of the automotive world.

After making several models – a 10-hp two-cylinder, a 15-hp three-cylinder and a 20-hp four-cylinder – in 1905 the new company made a 30-hp six-cylinder model. Then in 1906 the company laid down a one-model policy, and a brand-new 40/50-hp, six-cylinder, 7046-cc model was shown to the public at the Motor Show, clad in a silver-aluminium body. The Silver Ghost was born. It was made, with very few changes in basic design, for 19 years, and was bought by kings and presidents, by the famous and the rich from all corners of the globe, acquired for its prestige and loved for its grace, its silence and its trouble-free longevity. Today, Rolls-Royce will inform visitors who often enquire where they house their product museum, that there is *no* Rolls-Royce museum. All their cars are still in working order!

Until 1907, when the first hint of recession was seen on the horizon, the motor industry had plunged onwards to what it firmly believed would be everlasting prosperity and progress, an age of freedom and mobility for everyone. When for the first time the sales figures for the industry sagged, few realized that for a time at least production had exceeded demand. It was the first of the motor industry's regular recessions, and led to much re-thinking and re-grouping.

A note from a European motoring journal in 1907 makes curiously modern reading: 'A few years ago everybody wanted cars, regardless of cost, and with continuous fresh improvements; many took to buying cars every year, selling off the old.

Above: Stanley Steamer in commercial guise, made in Newton, Massachusetts, U.S.A. Steam power was favoured in that country by many in the early twentieth century. The last Stanley was made in 1927.

Top right: This 1905 Daimler 'Detachable' had hooks on top of its roof so that it could be winched off, converting the car to an open tourer.

Right: Standard 1907, when the word meant that the car was made to a high standard, not built down to a price! This fine 30 hp car has luxury *Roi des Belges* coachwork.

Below: The Rolls-Royce Silver Ghost was first seen at the 1906 Motor Show in London. The 40/50 hp Ghost had a 7-litre engine and a 4-speed overdrive gearbox, and was made for 19 years. The car seen here – the original model – is still in excellent working order.

Built by Napier in 1908 to the orders of a racing driver, this four-cylinder model was called a Hutton (Napier were promoting their six-cylinder cars at the time). The car created several Brooklands speed records.

'This golden age could not last. Customers soon discovered that the annual cost of a car was not only excessive but unnecessary and there was a general tendency to prefer comfort to speed. There was a considerable falling off in orders, and as the trade has gone on manufacturing, there is at present heavy surplus production. . . .' and the article goes on to say that numbers of French companies would succumb, and that their demise would consolidate the industry. We have heard similar sentiments many times since those relatively carefree Edwardian days.

In Britain the motor industry had centred mainly around the Midlands – Coventry, Birmingham, Wolverhampton – and workers had flocked to the region as they had flocked to the Lancashire mills a century earlier. Companies were formed, like Standard (1903), Singer (1905) and Hillman (1907) that were to offer solid and reliable material to the growing hordes of would-be owners, companies that would supply two generations of family motorists. On the luxury scale, Napier had firmly established their 'Six', largely by competition success, and of course Rolls-Royce was capturing the aristocratic market with Henry's Ghost, clothed in majesty by Barker, Mulliner and other eminent coach-builders.

Middle-of-the-road Riley were turning out 2-litre V-twins which looked a little like the round-radiator classic of France, the Delaunay-Belleville; only a year earlier in 1907, the Coventry company had been making crude tri-cars, three-wheelers not far removed from motorcycle design. Alldays were another with a product a cut above the popular markets, as were of course Daimler (now firmly wedded to their Royal clients, the British Monarchy) and the social-climbing Rover.

By 1910 cyclecar fever had hit Britain – and indeed all Europe – and many a motorcycle-engined, wire-and-bobbin bolide was seen weaving along the highway to the hazard of occupants and watchers alike.

Probably influenced by the light-car racing that was beginning to attract larger audiences, and certainly influenced by the desire of the lower-incomed man-in-the-street to have some sort of a four-wheeled motorcar – any sort as long as he could boast family mobility – shoals of cyclecars were pouring on to the unsuspecting market. To be fair, some were made with a degree of care, particularly the British three-wheeler made by H. F. S. Morgan in Malvern, Worcestershire. His first was powered by a V-twin unit from an abandoned motorcycle which he put into a light, tubular, three-wheeled chassis. Today the small factory at Malvern still painstakingly produces Morgans, now classic sportscars built in traditional style.

Another well-known pioneer of this dubious era was the Paris-made Bedelia, which, steered by a centre-pivot system and belt driven, looked about as roadworthy as a speedboat with its two seats arranged in tandem, one in front of the other. It suited the young, impecunious French sportsman however, and sold in large numbers. By 1912 over 40 different makes of cyclecar were shown at the Olympia Motor Show, ranging from the one-seater Rollo at 75 guineas to the tiny spidery GN which in time became the highly sporting Frazer-Nash.

From the cyclecar episode of motoring history came the light cars of immediate pre-war days. William Morris in England offered his first Morris-Oxford light car in 1913, and the little 10-hp, 1018-cc two-seater pioneered the so-called 'New Motoring's' graduation from the cyclecar era into respectability. Others joined Morris (as rivals rather than collaborators), in making cars that were genuine four-wheel pieces of engineering, rather than motorcycles with ideas above their station. Slightly larger than the first Morris was the Singer, a 1096-cc light car that had its gearbox housed in its back axle – and which inspired young Lionel Martin, who was looking for a car that he could tune up to high performance for competition, to build his first car in 1913, the car he dubbed Aston Martin. Peugeot of France offered the Bugatti-designed, 856-cc Bébé, another diminutive and simple car that exactly suited the new car-buying public.

The larger cars of the period were changing rapidly in appearance. Flatsided bodies and torpedo shapes (open four-seaters with a continuous line from the bonnet [hood] along the tops of the doors to the rear end) were becoming popular. On the other hand, weather protection was also being considered seriously for the first time. One foreign nobleman astounded the motoring circles by having the driving compartment of his landaulette enclosed by glass screens to protect his chauffeur from the

Alfa before Romeo. The first Alfas were made in Milan (at an old Darracq works) in 1910. This is the original model, a 4·1-litre, 24 hp open tourer.

elements, a design that was the fore-runner of the genuine *conduite intérieure*, as the French still tend to call a saloon or sedan. Tyres too began to play a part in protecting the passenger from the worst of the roads' ruts-and-bumps. Large-section tyres were used and pressures reduced in an effort to increase comfort. Electric lights were still very new, as were pressed steel wings [fenders], replacing the metal, wood and leather of yore, and pressed steel wheels.

The first practical self-starter was seen in 1912. American Charles Kettering, an electric motor expert working for Henry Leland's Cadillac Motor Car Company at Detroit, Michigan, had developed a motor that could generate enough energy over a short time to turn a heavy engine fast enough to spark it into life. The impact of this was greater than expected. Almost immediately a legion of new motorists appeared – lady drivers. Once the back-breaking necessity of turning the weighty and sometimes dangerous crank handle to start the engine had been overcome, the way was open for the woman at the wheel. The electric self-starter and lighting system became a standard fitting to the 5½-litre, 60-mph Cadillac of 1912, bringing about new body styling (elegance to suit a lady purchaser), new colours, a new advertising approach, and not least a new freedom for women, who could now undertake motoring journeys on their own without being considered indelicate or 'fast'. Before the following year was out most U.S. models were fitted with self-starters, although European manufacturers were slower to appreciate the advantages. Many of their clients already had self-starters. . .called chauffeurs.

THE AMAZING T

The greatest impact in the history of the automobile was made by the Ford phenomenon in the years before the First World War. Henry had started the Ford Motor Company in 1903 after a couple of false starts and was, by 1907, standing on the brink of the greatest development in motoring, his Model T, which was scheduled to be offered to an eager public in October 1908. 'Homely as a burro and useful as a pair of shoes' ran the advertisement, and they flocked for their new mechanical burro, buying more than 10,000 of them in the first production year – and continuing to buy the Model T until sales figures reached a fantastic 2 million a year during 1923–5.

The power for this little workhorse was a 20-hp, four-cylinder, three-bearing unit cast with an integral water-jacket and detachable cylinder-

Below: Riley of Britain made this 1907 V-twin two-seater, their first genuine car. Earlier the Coventry firm had produced tri-cars but in 1904 had moved to four-wheelers.

Right: Rover had made pedal cycles, progressed to motor cycles, and in 1904 made their first car, an 8 hp single-cylinder model. This is a 1907 example.

head. Its somewhat tricky planetary transmission had just two forward speeds and was designed to prevent too much damage being done to the gears by ham-fisted farm boys from Ploughsville. Capable of 45 mph and about 20 miles to the gallon, the Model T, the loved and derided 'Tin Lizzie', rapidly became part of the American scene in the days before the First World War.

Used in the city by salesmen and doctors (the first to appreciate its value) and down on the farm or ranch by country folk, the Model T offered not only utilitarian transport but could be adapted for sawing logs, hauling loads out of ditches, even milking cows. And when Ford moved into a new 60-acre factory and introduced modern mass production methods, the Model T was way out in front of any other motor maker in the world, using one-sixth of the nation's automotive labour force and producing one-half of the American nation's cars. Ford stock made fortunes for the lucky investors who had placed their faith and their

cash in the company. James Couzens, for instance, had put up $100 when the company started. He drew out $95,000 in dividends and in 1919 sold his shares for no less than $260,000.

While Henry Ford was building his automotive empire, W. C. Durant was playing out a similar drama with a number of other motor companies in the United States. The difference was that Durant was an entrepreneur, an ace salesman, rather than an engineer, although he had earlier built buggies for the U.S. market. His undoubted talents lay in persuasion and in organization. But his great energy, or his over-enthusiasm, eventually led him into trouble. Guided by Durant, the companies of Buick, Oldsmobile, Oakland (now Pontiac) and Cadillac formed the nucleus of what was to be called General Motors in 1908, a conglomerate designed to produce automobiles that would satisfy all

Below left: The sportive Hispano-Suiza Alfonso of 1912. Although the first cars were made in Spain from 1904, the company's Paris assembly plant sold well and the marque became thought of as a French product. Later, cars were manufactured in Paris.

Left: The French company of Sizaire-Naudin made single-cylinder cars long after most makers had moved to multi-cylinder products. However, the car had introduced many technical innovations.

sections of the market. He had originally tried to include Ford in his far-reaching plans but Henry proved too awkward a cuss for him and the deal fell through.

Durant bought everything in sight during the first couple of years of General Motors – accessory makers, electrical companies, parts manufacturers and a bag of smaller concerns like Elmore, Ranier, Rapid, Welsh and other sideliners. Durant built, in just two years, a group that looked impressive and indeed was a breathtaking example of empire-building, but there were too many rotten apples in his barrel and the new group descended into chaos. Henry Leland of the respected company of Cadillac bailed him out. Later, other names, some still familiar, were added to the General Motors stable – Chevrolet, Fisher Bodies, AC Spark Plugs, Frigidaire.

Above: Lanchester 1913. An English pioneer from the dawn of the industry, the marque was always ahead of its time. This car had a 36 hp six-cylinder engine and seated five.

William Richard Morris had repaired cycles in the 1890s and started to design cars in 1911. This is his first, the Morris Oxford Bullnose of 1913.

MEANWHILE...EUROPE

The golden years of European motoring were brought to a sudden halt soon after a Duke was shot and killed. The car in which Archduke Franz Ferdinand of Austria and his wife met their end was a Gräf und Stift, a car of humble origins – its makers were former cycle repairers in Vienna – but which had become known, over the 20 years of its life, as the Rolls-Royce of Austria (a title which tends to confirm the British company's supremacy as much as anything else) and which was perforce one of the historic cars of its time.

But the half-dozen years leading up to that tragic event, the moment in history that can be pinpointed as the end of an era and the beginning of the conflict that changed all our pasts and our futures, produced a number of fine pieces of personal transport for the wealthy few, and an increasing number of more utilitarian vehicles for others who until then would not have known the pleasure of owning any private transport more elaborate than a pedal cycle.

In 1912 Britain showed the short-nosed, 38-hp, six-cylinder Lanchester at its motor show, now a regular annual event that was part of the motoring scene, and the already legendary Prince Henry Vauxhall (chassis only: £495). In 1913 a 10-hp, four-cylinder AC made its debut; the Surrey-based company had been making funny little hansom-cabby, three-wheeler 'sociables' until then. The same year also saw a car, subsequently made for almost ten years, that well illustrated the changes that had swiftly come about in the design of, and attitude to the new age of motoring, and pointed the way to the changes about to take place...the Sunbeam, an immensely successful touring car, designed by Breton engineer Louis Coatalen who had worked successfully for Humber and Hillman. A designer who built and raced the cars he dreamed up, Coatalen was a man for all seasons for his company and was the mainspring of Sunbeam's illustrious reputation of later years.

44

Other models – the large Napier saloon for example – showed how coachwork design had at last broken free of traditional horse-carriage influence, with its low lines and enclosed bodywork that provided complete cover for the driver as well as 'paying' passengers. On most cars one saw clean and simple electric lighting by 1914, and detachable wheels had cut out some of the frightful problems of changing tyres after the still-inevitable puncture. Brass was slowly disappearing and the trend towards using the car as an instrument of daily labour was more evident in those last pre-war days.

French designs had confirmed that the single cylinder was now dead (the Sizaire-Naudin had made a 'one-lunger' until 1910, stepping up power over the years by enlarging the diameter then the stroke of its lonely piston). A single (monoblock) casting for the cylinders was now normal, doing away with much of the copper spaghetti and nuts-and-bolts of earlier designs. Split-V screens were seen, and the overhanging saloon roof which acted as a sort of sunvisor for the driver was fashionable, as were open, square-cut, torpedo-tourer shapes. A Lancia Theta could be bought with a flowing moulded landaulette or sedan body with lines that belonged to a decade later; the Peugeot Bébé of the day was surprisingly similar in profile to Austin's Seven of nearly ten years later; Itala of Turin made a tourer that looked like the great tourers of the Twenties, as did the British Valveless, and the small French Sigma (a modest 'assembled' car) had the distinct appearance of post-war build.

Coal-shovel bonnets [hoods] abounded in France as Renault took over the lead in popular production, and many a wise competitor copied the unorthodox Renault front end. From diminutive Decauville to majestic Delaunay-Belleville (with its round-bellied radiator similar to the Dutch Spyker), protection from the weather had assumed paramount importance, and by 1914 large glass areas surrounded the passengers and chaffeur alike. Motoring clothing, up to then a vital part of the traveller's

Last of an era – a 1913 Sunbeam tourer. The British company had started life back in the nineteenth century enamelling tinware, had moved into bicycle making and thence to cars.

wardrobe – goatskin great-coats with the fur exposed or racoon coats, dust veils, masks and so on – were at last thrown into the attic to become sought-after relics half a century later.

The so-called Edwardian period was one of rapid advances of fundamentals during its early stages, and of increasingly sophisticated refinements during the last year before the First World War. The car was not yet a completely accepted method of transport for the work of the world, but progress in engine mechanics, in suspension, in bodywork and, most importantly, in manufacture, had brought the automobile to the brink of modern usage as a functional artifact with an essential role to play in everyday life.

The Years Between the Wars

If Herbert Austin had produced only his Seven of 1922 he would still have made history. The diminutive Austin Seven brought motoring to an eager post-First World War public.

The period immediately following the ending of hostilities in 1918 was a turbulent one in which the scramble to turn swords into ploughshares was frustrated by post-war shortages, inflation (the like of which has probably not been seen since) and labour difficulties.

A four-year war of attrition in which virtually every major nation in the world was involved – and many of the smaller ones too – with all the waste of raw materials which that involved, meant that many of the larger manufacturers simply could not obtain the steel and other commodities they required to maintain output at a rate which would make their war-inflated factories economic to run.

The cost of the war in terms of men and materials meant that the average British car of 1919 cost practically double the figure of its 1914 counterpart, and increases of this nature were reflected in all other spheres. Initially, this doubling in price did not deter potential buyers, for there was a desperate shortage of cars, but when the supply situation eased by the end of 1920, prices began to fall again.

Many of the larger manufacturers were still in a difficult position, however. Ordered into munitions initially, and producing nothing else for four years, many were surprised by the Armistice, and caught with no new models 'on the drawing board' and with many machine tools either unsuitable for peacetime production or worn out from constant use.

America's involvement in the war, although massive at the end, came later, and consequently she had expanded her markets considerably between 1914 and 1916 and up until her own entry into the war in 1917. She therefore had a three-year start, more up-to-date models and many new customers who had been wooed away from British, French and German manufacturers during the years that those countries had ceased manufacture for civilian consumption.

This then was the scene at the beginning of the post-war period, and at first, when the big battalions were re-converting their factories and generally girding their loins to meet post-war demand, many small newcomers hopefully joined their ranks. These firms offered an assort-ment of 'assembled' cars to a public who were desperate for transport of any kind. Many were poorly designed and constructed and most of them relied upon specialist outside suppliers for their engines, gearboxes, axles and other major components.

Below: Aircraft-maker Gabriel Voisin had a dislike of any design that was not strictly functional, a taste that showed itself in the strangely angular shape of his cars. This is a Voisin C3 tourer of 1923.

Right: One of the great Mercedes-Benz line of the Twenties, the 7·1-litre SSK, the short-chassis version of the SS, both of which, although called sports-tourers won Grand Prix events against pure racing vehicles. The SSK developed 225 bhp in supercharged form.

A steam-lorry maker once said that his vehicles lacked the 'thump' of his Bentley as it loped down the road – and Bugatti called them the fastest lorries ever made. But the Bentleys of the Twenties, often known by their labels, Green, Blue, Red, were greatly loved British sports cars.

In America particularly the assembled car enjoyed a longer life than across the Atlantic, and literally hundreds of firms mushroomed during the Twenties. On both sides of the water, however, while many of the newcomers had a history of general engineering and war work in munitions, as many again had no engineering background whatever. Canned soup, government surplus and vending machine distributors were just a few of those trying their hands (usually unsuccessfully) at motor manufacture during this period.

There were others though, particularly those who had been engaged in the aircraft industry – which had greatly expanded during the war – who turned their new technology to good advantage in peacetime. Salmson of Billancourt, France, for example, had been renowned for their water-cooled and later air-cooled radial aero engines, and in 1919 they entered the arena of motor manufacture by the simple expedient of taking out a manufacturing licence for the GN cyclecar, already being produced in England. This rapidly developed into a fully-fledged small sportscar of the type which dominated the French scene throughout the Twenties. Initially a rather unorthodox little design incorporating a differential-less rear axle and a four-cylinder engine with a single pushrod per cylinder which also operated the inlet valves as a *pull* rod! Salmson's first 'home-grown' design was the work of Emil Petit. He later developed it into a twin overhead cam unit of remarkable efficiency and speed, but still of only 1100-cc capacity and with a two-bearing crankshaft. In this form, a Salmson won the 1921 Cyclecar Grand Prix and took second place (ironically behind a British GN) in the Brooklands 220-mile Race.

As if all this was not enough, first and second places were taken in both events in 1922. The sporting character of the Salmson was assured and the zenith of its career was achieved in 1927 with second and third places

in the general classification at Le Mans.

Touring model Salmsons acquired the overhead camshaft engine in 1922 but towards the end of the decade the small sports car vogue in France disappeared virtually overnight, and the arrival of the cheap MG Midget on the British market killed what British sales might have kept the type alive after 1929.

THE LUXURY MARKET

Also located at Billancourt, the Farman brothers had made their reputation with aero engines, and the design of the 1920 6·6-litre A6B Farman reflected this background. Much use was made of aluminium alloy in the construction of the engine, valves were actuated by a single overhead camshaft, and the cars boasted a peculiar suspension system combining a single transverse spring with two cantilevers.

Apart from the upstairs camshaft, Farmans bore no resemblance to their neighbours, Salmson, and were designed wholly for the luxury market. Whereas Salmson's licence-produced GN had sold some 3,000 examples by 1921, Farman's total production up to 1931 was a less than impressive 120, and it is remarkable that any should have survived from such a small output. In fact, about four or five are preserved today.

Built in exactly the same idiom and aiming at an identical market, the H6B Hispano-Suiza announced in 1919 at the Paris Salon was the first French-developed Hispano model and, at first, no faster than the Farman. However, it was hailed as the sensation of the show, and boasting four wheel brakes five years before Rolls-Royce grudgingly gave them to the Silver Ghost, the car was equally at home with sporting bodywork or bespoke formal coachwork, and was powered by an engine identical in capacity to that of the Farman.

The Vauxhall 30/98 (it was never discovered why the car was given this name) was the company's most successful sports car. Produced until 1926 it was used extensively as a competition vehicle, but was flexible enough to be used as a family car.

Often called the 'Baby Lincoln' – it looked a little like its more expensive cousin – the 200 cu in Model A Ford, introduced in 1928, was the successor of the Model T.

The Hispano-Suiza's fixed cylinderhead was a somewhat archaic feature, but otherwise the design was advanced, being one half of a V-12 aero engine developed during the war but never used. With a seven-bearing, pressure-fed crankshaft and a single overhead camshaft operating two valves per cylinder, the engine gave 135 bhp at 3,000 rpm, combining a good power-to-weight ratio with first class reliability in the best traditions of aero practice.

So flexible was the engine that it could be accelerated from 10 km/h to 80 km/h (6 mph to 50 mph) *in top gear* in only 21 seconds, a feature aided by superb performance and handling. Admittedly it was not quite so quiet in operation as other luxury marques – a fact which probably contributed to a preponderance of sports models having survived – but its success with the 'carriage trade' was sufficient to give Rolls-Royce a severe shaking.

Down at Issy-les-Moulineaux, pioneer aviator Gabriel Voisin had built some 10,000 aircraft, mainly for the military, by the time the Armistice was signed, and he entered the motor industry in much the same way as Salmson had done, by taking over someone else's design. In Voisin's case it was to André Citroën that he turned, taking over the manufacturing rights of a Citroën design which Citroën himself had never used. The 18-hp, four-cylinder utilized the double sleeve-valve Knight 4-litre engine and was produced as the C1 Voisin. Henceforward, Voisin became wedded to sleeve-valve engines, and consistently developed them to a high degree.

The Voisin was a first class motorcar, capable eventually in C1 form of 130 km/h (80 mph), and numbered many titled owners among its customers. Voisin bodywork frequently combined aviation construction techniques with Voisin's own eccentricities to produce a strange mixture of practicality and uncompromising ugliness, and doubtless some of his more bizarre designs contributed to customer resistance.

BENTLEY DAYS

Such was the spate of newcomers to the manufacturing scene that the Olympia Motor Shows of both 1919 and 1920 overspilled to the White City Stadium, and relegated to this overspill in 1920, three newcomers shared adjoining stands. They were representative of the three major

Ford halted production of the T in May 1927, just after the 15-millionth example had rolled out of the works. This Tudor (2-door) one of the last of the line.

categories of new make to be found on both sides of the Atlantic during this period; one of the three was destined to achieve immortality, the other two, obscurity.

Stand 426 housed Bentley Motors of Cricklewood, who had already shown their new 3-litre model at the 1919 show. Famous for his wartime aero engines, 'W. O.' Bentley had pre-war experience of the motor trade importing DFP cars (and competing with them) and the Bentley radiator owed more than a passing resemblance to the DFP.

Like the Hispano, the 3-litre Bentley relied upon a fixed head and single overhead camshaft and developed about 70 hp in its early guise. Only 1,600 were made, and yet the whole concept of motoring in the Twenties conjures up a picture of an open-bodied Bentley roaring open-throated down a tree-lined, straight, unmetalled road, driven by a University-scarved young man accompanied by a slip of a girl with an Eton-crop hairstyle and a cloche hat.

If the small sports car was the exclusive province of the French until the advent of the MG Midget, then the long stroke fast tourer represented the British scene, and the Bentley was the epitome of the fast tourer. Other makes emulated it, like the HE from Reading, and there were Continental counterparts in the Type 51 Itala (which distinguished itself in competition from the Targa Florio in Italy to the Aspendale Track in Australia) and the D1 Delage, at 2·1 litres smaller than the Bentley but in sports form utilizing the aluminium pistons for which Bentley was also famous.

Offered in short and long chassis form as the Red Label and Blue Label respectively, the Bentley 3-litre was supplemented in 1926 by the 6½-litre, six-cylinder model, the intention being to capture a proportion of the available carriage trade. The attempt was unsuccessful but not wasted, since it resulted in the 180 hp 'Speed Six' of 1929 which is considered by many to be the best model Bentley ever designed, and which was responsible for the last two Le Mans wins – Barnato/Clement in 1929 and Barnato/Kidston in 1930.

The 3-litre Bentley had developed into the 4½-litre by 1927, still a four-cylinder model but with sufficient potential for its 100 hp to be increased to 130 hp before production ended, and won Le Mans in the hands of Barnato and Rubin in 1928. Fielded in supercharged form (of which 'W. O.' himself did not wholly approve) by Sir Henry 'Tim' Birkin and

A French car with a sporting and quality reputation, the Delage was produced from 1905 to 1954. This is a 1927-8 2·1-litre Delage DIS/6 tourer.

51

developing 182 hp, a 4½-litre took second place in the *formule libre* French Grand Prix of 1930.

Bentley's final significant car was the superb 8-litre six. Only 100 were built before Bentley went bankrupt in the summer of 1931. Had it not been for this last model (which presented a considerable threat to Rolls-Royce at the top end of the market) it is debatable if Rolls-Royce would have bid for the company.

THE EVERYMAN CLASSICS

Well-known motorcycle makers Clyno of Wolverhampton started later in the day than most, in 1922, and produced an excellent 'assembled' car for Mr. Everyman which ran William Morris and his 'Bullnosed' Cowleys and Oxfords a close second for a few seasons. Morris was the more

An American with a distinguished pedigree, this 1933 Packard V12 convertible-Victoria Model 1006 had bodywork by Dietrich (Owner A.F. Mirremiar).

successful of the two however, and was the first manufacturer to break the 40,000 units a year barrier. Unfortunately Clyno elected to enter into a price war with Morris, sacrificed quality for quantity, and lost the battle.

Quite apart from the small-fry, however, the established manufacturers did not all have a smooth ride in post-war years. Austin, in business on his own account since 1906, made a bad mistake in concentrating all his post-war production energies initially upon a single model, the Twenty. Excellent car it may have been, but it was nudging the luxury class, and with post-war inflation, too expensive for the mass market for which Austin's factories were geared.

A versatile engineer, Austin introduced the Heavy Twelve as a supplementary model in 1921. Initially with a 1661-cc side-valve engine and a later enlarged to 1861-cc, this model proved virtually indestructible

and remained in production in taxicab form into the late Forties. It contributed as much, if not more, to the post-war recovery of Austin as did the famous little Austin Seven.

The brainchild of Herbert Austin himself, the Seven was conceived at a time when the fortunes of the parent company were at a low ebb and, so it is said, Herbert – known universally in the works as 'Pa' – would disappear for long solo runs on his bicycle rather than face the bank on paydays! As his Board of Directors was unimpressed with his plans for a new baby car, Austin borrowed the services of a young draughtsman and set up a drawing office in the billiard room of his own home.

The result was the Seven, announced to the Press in 1922, and intended primarily to appeal to the family man who wanted something better than a motorcycle combination, did not fancy a crude cyclecar, and could not afford a full size motor car. Like Bugatti's Peugeot Bébé of a decade earlier, the Austin Seven was in effect a large car in miniature, and combined all the virtues of a large car – water-cooled, four-cylinder engine, gearbox and live axle – with an economy of operation and low price. It was an immediate best-seller, and continued to find an appreciative market for the following 17 years.

Still at the popular end of the market, the dominant force during the Twenties was Ford, firmly entrenched at River Rouge in Detroit, and with an assembly plant at Trafford Park in Manchester, England dating from 1911, with various other assembly operations throughout the world. His staple offering (in fact, the only model available) since 1908 was the Model T, an extremely cheap, husky, four-cylinder car with a reputation for reliability with minimal maintenance which had passed into legend.

Beloved by Henry Ford and cursed by two generations of motorists for those aspects of its design which Henry steadfastly refused to update, the Model T soldiered on until 1927, by which time it was running a poor second to Chevrolet in the sales race. Finally Ford characteristically shut down the whole plant while a new model was prepared, and after seven months of apparent inactivity, rumours of impending bankruptcy were rife.

The new car appeared in 1928. The Model A was a solidly-built workhorse with pleasing lines and a radiator design borrowed from the luxury Lincoln which Ford had purchased when Henry Leland ran into financial difficulties in 1922. Over 633,000 were sold in 1928, and 1,507,132 Model As found customers in 1929, re-establishing Ford's lead over Chevrolet.

Chevrolet themselves had started modestly in 1911 when, together with racing driver Louis Chevrolet, William Durant brought out a 4·9-litre with side valves in a T-head. This was followed in 1916 by the '490' (the name was taken straight off the price tag), a four-cylinder overhead valve four costing only $490. In 1917 sales totalled a healthy 70,701 units and in that year General Motors acquired the company. Billy Durant went on to form yet another empire as Durant Motors, and this subsequently embraced Locomobile, Flint, Rugby and Star as well as his low-priced and initially best selling Durant Four.

U.S. LUXURY PRODUCTS

Spiritual home of the mass-produced car America may have been, but it would be quite wrong to imagine that she relied totally upon foreign

Bottom: One of the classic cars of the Auburn-Cord-Duesenberg Museum in Auburn, Indiana, U.S.A., is this 1935 Auburn boat-tail Speedster. The 150 bhp models were guaranteed to have been tested up to 100 mph.

Below: Alfa Romeo 2·6 litres, a sporting aristocrat from Milan. Vittorio Jano's 8C 2300 supercharged Alfa Romeo had appeared in 1931 and had won four Le Mans in a row, and three Mille Miglias.

imports to satisfy home demand for luxury vehicles. Although popularly associated with cheap Fords, Dodges, Chevrolets and Overlands – chiefly because these constituted the bulk of American exports to the rest of the world – America espoused some of the best built classic designs to grace either road or race track.

At Indianapolis, home of the hallowed brick racetrack, Fred and Augie Duesenberg at first built racing cars – their Bugatti-inspired 3-litre straight-eight with overhead camshaft and three vertical valves won the French Grand Prix in 1921 and their first production car was unveiled at the end of 1920. Generally accepted as being the first American production straight-eight, the Duesenberg Model A was not only extremely advanced, it was also decidely expensive.

Generally acknowledged, together with Peerless and Pierce-Arrow, to be the Rolls-Royce of America, Packard were fielding a twin-six (the world's first series production car with this configuration) in 1920, as their sole offering, but this was in turn joined by a side valve single-six

Below: Aston Martin's 1½-litre long-chassis model had a classic front end – in this case well covered with stone guards, common in the days of rougher roads.

Above: The Duesenburg Model J had an eight-cylinder, 6·9-litre Lycoming engine that developed 265 bhp; double that of its nearest rival. Seen here is a 1929 Dual-cowl Phaeton.

which remained in production until 1928 and which was responsible for the majority of Packard sales.

Connersville, Indiana was the stamping ground of the luxury McFarlan, the reputation of which has grown out of all proportion to the number of cars actually sold. At most, 235 cars a year were produced (and frequently less), yet the McFarlan was typical of all that was best among buyers of bespoke motorcars. The TV (Twin-Valve) Model utilized a massive engine embodying no less than three ignition systems involving the use of 18 sparking plugs, and at $9,000 the Knickerbocker Cabriolet was one of the most expensive American cars of the period.

Oakland, California however, enjoyed the distinction of being the home of one of the largest – and almost certainly one of the most expensive – American makes. At 13½-litres and giving 125 hp, the Fageol was priced from $9,500 (for a bare chassis) to $17,000 complete.

It would not be fair to deal with America's luxury makes without some mention of the American Rolls-Royce, although the Springfield, Massachusetts-built cars were never totally successful in the commercial sense. Unlike their British counterparts, they were offered complete with bodywork if the customer so wished. In addition, custom bodies were built by outside firms including the established and respected house of Brewster, whose bodies can be found on many of the 1703 examples of

Silver Ghosts and 1241 Phantom 1s built in the American plant.

As in pioneer days the development of the American car during the Twenties did not follow exactly the same pattern as Europe, and just as the high-wheeler was a typically American phenomenon in the mid-Edwardian period, so the persistence of the steam car – with a mild revival in 1923–4 – was peculiarly American. Even the old-fashioned Stanley managed sales of some 600 per year up until 1925 (the last cars were made in 1927), and perfectionist Abner Doble was offering his advanced steamers until 1931.

Still leading the luxury field at home in England, and despite the inroads made into the bespoke field by Hispano-Suiza, Isotta-Fraschini and the American Cadillac, Rolls-Royce persisted with the now ageing Silver Ghost – still basically a 1906 design. Then in 1922, the Ascot racing fraternity, picnicking with a Fortnum hamper and a bottle of Bollinger, were appalled to find themselves confronted by a 'Baby' Rolls – The Twenty. Rolls had produced an economy car!

Below: *Traction Avant* was the French name for it – the 1934 front-wheel drive 7CV Citröen that was years in advance of most cars of its day.

Beloved of nouveau riche and war profiteers (*Punch* called them post-war sportsmen), the Twenty was frowned upon by the Establishment when first announced, in the event quite unfairly. None of the standards with which the larger car had become associated were sacrificed in the smaller model, and with its monobloc engine, overhead valves and central gearchange it was a decided improvement over the Ghost in many respects. The arrival of the New Phantom (Phantom I) for the 1926 season silenced the critics, although many felt that no worthy successor to the Ghost had been found until the advent of the Phantom II in 1929.

From the mid-Twenties the wind of change had been blowing strongly, and the first casualties, no matter how long-established they may have been, were those who had consistently ignored the warning signals. The First World War had swept away half the crowned heads of Europe, and with them the wealth and estates of many of the old aristocratic families who had made up their courts. These were the traditional buyers of, at first, horsedrawn carriages and, later, luxury motorcars, and their disappearance struck many a mortal blow.

The celebrated Delaunay-Belleville, that round-radiatored symbol of Edwardian opulence from St. Denis, Paris, the car which had been dubbed the Gallic Rolls-Royce, was never the same after the fall of Russia to the Bolsheviks (the Tzar had kept a stable of Delaunays), and whilst

The Austro-Daimler of Vienna was originally an offspring of the German Daimler company. The ADR8 was its only eight-cylinder car, built between 1930 and 1933.

they survived the Depression and staggered on through the Thirties utilizing American and German engines, the malady which beset them dated from the First World War.

Many other old-established companies were similarly afflicted, particularly in Belgium, once the home of proud makers like Excelsior and Pipe. Both of these succumbed in 1932, and even FN survived only on the strength of their ordnance division during the rearmament of the Thirties.

Towards the end of the Twenties there was a growing demand for cheap saloon-bodied cars. Mr. Everyman was tired of struggling in the pouring rain with one-man hoods which needed six hands, and all-weather equipment which wasn't – and in America Dodge, with their all-steel saloon, and Essex with their enclosed 'Coach' had shown the way.

The day of the composite bodybuilder was on its way out, and makers of cheaper cars were finding that they had to be comfortable, reliable and easy to operate if they were to remain competitive. Inevitably rationalization won the day, and despite his worries about unemployment, the average family man in the early Thirties obtained a far better deal when he bought a new car than ever before.

William Morris led the way with his £100 Morris Minor in 1929, and although his open two-seater with its rather complicated overhead camshaft engine was not too successful, it implanted the idea of a £100 car in everyone's head, and it was Ford, pioneer of cost-cutting whilst maintaining quality, who offered the first £100 saloon, the Y type two-door Popular, in 1935.

By this time, Ford's British Trafford Park assembly plant had given way to a purpose-built factory on reclaimed marshland at Dagenham in Essex, opened in 1932, and the Y type was not only the first truly British Ford, it was absolutely right for the economic climate of the day.

Austin's Seven, updated as the streamlined Ruby, was still giving good service and keeping the factory fully employed; it was also offered, in two-seater form, at £100. For those who wanted something a little larger, the Ten introduced in 1932 was a best-seller. Morris hit the jackpot in 1935 with his Series One 'Eight'. The accent of the day was on small, cheap cars, and even relatively small manufacturers like Jowett and Standard – the latter with their worm drive Nine – were able to weather the worst of the storm.

Most stylish American casualty of all was, perhaps, the mini-empire of Erret Lobban Cord, an entrepreneur *par excellence*, who having acquired control of Auburn – an old-established company – in 1924, proceeded to revamp its cars completely. Duesenberg came into the Cord fold in 1926, and Fred Duesenberg's first car for his new employer (Cord had stipulated it had to be new and quite exceptional) was the Model 'J' announced in 1928.

In looks, refinement, size, specification and speed it surpassed anything at that time being offered by other American manufacturers, and its Lycoming engine (Cord also owned Lycoming), a 6·9-litre eight and twin overhead camshafts and four valves per cylinder (quite unique for an American design) produced no less than 265 bhp, more than double its nearest rival.

In 1929 Cord optimistically produced a car under his own name. Designated the L-29, it was the first front-wheel-drive car to achieve anything like public acclaim and when it reappeared in redesigned form with a coffin-nosed body and disappearing headlights from the drawing board of Gordon Buehrig as the Model 810, it established a classic line which has since been acclaimed by bodies as far divorced from motoring

Above: The SS Jaguar of 1938 had a 3·5-litre ohv engine developing 125 bhp, an attractive and inexpensive sports-car of the Thirties, and direct ancestor of today's XJS.

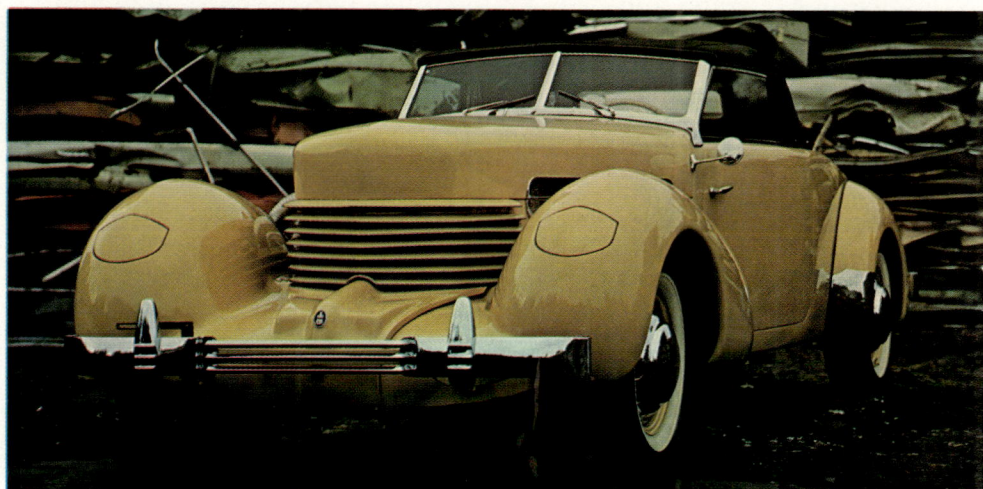

Left: The coffin-nose body and vanishing headlamps of the Cord 810 and 812 of the mid-Thirties plus its vivid 4·7-litre V8 (supercharged in this 812) made it a memorable car.

Vincenzo Lancia's Lambda appeared in 1922, introducing new methods of construction. This is a 1929 S1 model (somewhat modified) that once belonged to the Italian dictator Mussolini.

as the Design Council and the Museum of Modern Art.

The demise of the Cord empire in 1937 (when the worst of the Depression was over) remains one of the ironies of the period. Cord's elegant and advanced cars enlivened those dark days, and have deservedly achieved the stature of all-time classics.

Cord was not alone in espousing front-wheel-drive, however. André Citroën, most successful of all the newcomers in 1919, popularized it with his 7CV 'Traction Avant' in 1934. A design demanding a completely new factory, the car was an instant success and remained in production until succeeded by the equally iconoclastic DS19 in 1955. The expense of the factory and retooling forced Citroën to sell out to Michelin, however. Such is the penalty of being ahead of one's time.

Although the British Alvis company's venture into front-wheel-drive was abortive, they made a most successful transition from the out-and-out sports car of the Twenties to the fast and stylish drophead coupes, tourers and sporting saloons which characterized their output during the Thirties. The Speed Twenty, and the later Speed Twentyfive were good looking, fast enough, comfortable, and handled and stopped well. In these attributes they echoed their contemporaries – the Derby-built 3½- and 4½-litre Bentleys, the flexible and low-slung Meadows-powered Invicta, the SS Jaguars, forerunners of today's XJS, and even the large and luxurious Austro-Daimler.

For the traditionalist, sports car *aficionados* could still buy a chain-drive Frazer-Nash up until 1939 (although the company were importing BMWs from 1934 onwards), or a three-wheeler Morgan (latterly with a Ford four-cylinder engine). The Thirties also heralded the arrival of the synchromesh gearbox, a refinement and ease of operation never dreamed of by motorists in 1919.

In Italy and Germany, Fascist governments saw, in Alfa-Romeo and Mercedes-Benz respectively, the means whereby nationalistic fervour could be encouraged through the medium of international motor sport, and both factories, together with Auto Union, received massive subsidies. In the case of Mercedes and Auto Union, these had the effect of making the German teams virtually unbeatable for a period, but in fairness, both Alfa and Mercedes had a respectable sporting pedigree, and the SS and SSK Mercedes series of the late Twenties and early Thirties are now acknowledged as some of the greatest sports car designs ever built.

Both Germany and Italy contributed a great deal to the advancement of the design of ordinary cars during the two decades, Lancia's Lambda pre-dating most of its contemporaries by more than a decade, and Germany absolutely bursting with innovation under the influence of engineers of the calibre of Porsche and Ganz. Independent suspension, development of two-stroke designs for motorcars, rear engines – all saw the light of day on a popular scale during the ten years leading up to the Second World War.

The twenty years 'between the wars' were robust, ever-changing, vital years in the development of the automobile, and the level of technology concerned with that development determined that the Second World War would be almost totally mechanized.

The New Generation (1950-1980)

British sporting classics. A 1973 1275 cc MG Midget and an MGB, with 1798 cc under the bonnet [hood], rest briefly in idyllic scenery.

The effects of the Second World War on the automobile manufacturers of the world were, in many ways, similar to those resulting from the 1914–18 conflict. As before, all had been diverted to war work, and similarly the rigours of war tested designs to the full, resulting in rapid developments and improvements. But there the similarity ceased.

Whilst the motor vehicle – and the aeroplane – had played an important part in the First World War, the Second World War was a war of far greater mobility both on the ground and in the air, and the growth of air power in particular was to replace, to a great extent, the concentration upon shells and other projectiles which had engaged so many manufacturers during 1914–18.

Civilian motor manufacture, which had been maintained at a trickle throughout the First World War, halted in Britain altogether in 1940 and, following the Japanese attack in 1941 on Pearl Harbour, in 1942 in America. Germany's motor industry had been cleverly rationalized by the state during the Thirties as a carefully orchestrated part of Germany's covert re-armament plans. Fewer companies were, however, diverted totally from vehicle production since there was a far greater need for trucks and general purpose vehicles, tanks, light gun carriers and half-track vehicles.

By 1939 the American automobile industry had been whittled down to

61

Designed in the late-Thirties but introduced in 1949, the diminutive Citröen 2CV was an ideal car for austere post-war days, and has been made ever since with few changes in fundamental concept.

just 18 makes of any significance, of which Chevrolet, Buick, Pontiac, Oldsmobile, and Cadillac-La Salle were controlled by General Motors; Ford controlled Lincoln-Mercury; Plymouth, Dodge, Chrysler and De Soto were all members of the Chrysler camp. This left only Willys-Overland, Studebaker, Packard, Hudson, Nash-Lafayette, Graham and Hupmobile independent, and the latter two were on their last legs.

In many respects, the war saved the American independents, and it certainly gave a new lease of life to Willys who, together with Ford, turned out hundreds of wartime Jeeps. This ultra-successful maid-of-all-work was, ironically, designed by the struggling Bantam company, originally formed to build the British Austin Seven under licence in America, but who had neither the facilities nor the capital to produce it in the numbers demanded by the military.

Such was the enormity of the 1939–45 conflict that it took civilian manufacturers quite a time to get back into stride. Even the Americans had only ageing 1942 designs to offer at first, with the exception of two, both significantly the very last to challenge the supremacy of Detroit mass production, for both Tucker and Kaiser were newcomers. The Tucker

A wartime maid-of-all-work, the Jeep, made by U.S. companies Ford and Willys. Now the GPW ¼-ton utility vehicle is a precious collector's item, after thousands were abandoned to scrap in the late-Forties. More than 635,000 Jeeps were made during the Second World War.

Torpedo, built in Chicago, Illinois was far ahead of its time, with padded dashboard, pop-out windscreen and front passenger crash compartment, disc brakes and flat-six, rear-mounted, water-cooled engine. After three stormy years, however, the project folded.

The Kaiser (and its sister car the Frazer) was built in the huge plant at Willow Run, Michigan, used for the mass-production of B-24 Liberator bombers. Remembered for their stylish and innovative designs, Kaiser lasted until 1954 when, having taken over Willys, they moved to Brazil as the Kaiser-Jeep Corporation.

The success story of the independents was surely Hudson and Nash, who together formed American Motors and showed the way towards the future in 1958 with the introduction of their first 'compact' car, considerably smaller than the huge, over-engined hippos which Detroit had been churning out since the war, and far more acceptable to European markets. It was a winner and, named the Rambler, sold

Successor to the Citröen *Traction Avant* of 1934, the equally advanced DS19 was first shown in 1955. Its front wheel drive and self-levelling suspension plus power-assistance for almost everything else caused a sensation.

Right: The motor industry's classic disaster? The Edsel, named after Henry Ford's son, was introduced in 1958 to fill a market gap that had vanished by the time it appeared. Production ceased late in 1959.

Below: Production of the Chrysler 'letter' range of cars started in 1955 with the 300 housing a V8 6½-litre unit. This is a 1960 300F a model with a number of NASCAR records to its credit.

486,000 units in 1960 to take American Motors into third place in the sales race, ahead of Chrysler's Plymouth.

American styling during the Fifties left much to be desired, and while engineering improvements saw the gradual disappearance of the straight-six in favour of the V-8 and increasing use of automatic transmissions, handling fell far behind European standards.

In Britain, post-war styling tended to be pure 1939 with bits tacked on. Separate wings and headlights and sit-up-and-beg bodywork were still the order of the day in 1946, together with petrol rationing and a quota

Right: Small Wonder. The VW Beetle changed little in appearance since it was first made in early post-war days. Its numbers outran the record 15 million Ford Model Ts and formed the basis for the sophisticated Porsche.

system which dictated that the majority of new cars went for export to earn much-needed foreign currency. Those who were lucky enough to be able not only to afford a new car but to obtain one before 1950, had then to sign a covenant that they would not re-sell it for two years.

Notable exceptions in the styling doldrums were, strangely, two firms who had previously been renowned for their conservative traditions. Armstrong-Siddeley had always occupied uneasily a market slot somewhere midway between Humber and the smaller Rolls models, and had advertised their pre-war 12 hp as being 'for the daughters of gentlemen', but by 1949 they boasted independent front suspension and were among the first to announce their post-war programme.

Jowett on the other hand, whilst remaining wed to their pre-war flat-four engine configuration, swept aside their agricultural image once and for all with a most attractive fast-back saloon, the Javelin, announced in 1947. At the time when everything else looked undeniably 1939-ish, it boasted unitary body-chassis construction, aerodynamic lines, all round independent suspension giving excellent handling, and a top speed of 80 mph. Garage mechanics complained that the front wheel had to be taken off to change a plug, but the class wins notched up by the make in the 1949 and 1951 Monte Carlo Rallies and at Le Mans in 1950, 1951 and 1952 silenced the critics.

Experience gained in motor sport (Jaguar won the Le Mans 24 Hours race no less than five times in the Fifties) has always been reflected in Jaguar production cars, a current model of which is this sleek 5343 cc V12 150-mph XJS.

The ubiquitous Mini. First seen in 1959 behind a Morris or an Austin badge, the tiny transverse-engined Mini soon gained a reputation of its own – mainly by winning almost any sport in which it competed.

THE POST-WAR WATERSHED

The year 1948 was in fact the watershed for post-war British design, heralding the introduction of the 'new line'. For manufacturers like Singer, Standard (with their Vanguard) and Austin this meant recessed headlights, integral wings [fenders] and a slabsidedness which owed much to Detroit and which did little to enhance appearances. It was, however, the first real step towards modernity, and while initially the new bodies often tended to cloak mechanics of pre-war origin (Singer's chain-driven overhead camshaft four dated from the late Twenties, and the new Morris Minor still utilized the pre-war side-valve eight) the trend was towards new engine designs as well as new styling.

Austin emerged as the dominant post-war giant. The merger of the two companies Austin and Morris to form the British Motor Corporation in 1952 was the logical outcome. Fitted with Austin's overhead valve A35 engine, the Morris Minor went from strength to strength and was not finally phased out until the Seventies.

Because Britain's bread-and-butter family cars were unsuitable for many overseas markets – particularly the United States – much of her exports to the U.S. in the early post-war years tended to be sports cars of the type for which Britain had become famous, and for which G.I.s stationed there during the war had acquired a taste. Of these, the 'T'

In 1976 Porsche offered a front-engined car, the 2-litre 924, for the first time in its history. The larger 4·5 928 appeared in 1978. This is the 924.

67

series MGs – the TD, TC and the TF – represented the logical development of the pre-war two-seater, and until 1956 they were largely responsible for the popularization of the British sports car in America.

But the old order was changing and in 1948 William Lyons, whose SS Jaguars had dominated the pre-war market for low priced yet stylish sports saloons and dropheads in Britain, introduced an entirely new sports model. Designated the XK 120 and boasting a twin cam 'six' of own manufacture, this revolutionary model incorporated all that was best in modern aerodynamics, and combined this with 160 bhp and a top speed in production form of 120 mph, at the very low price of £1,263.

An immediate success, it signalled the development of the post-war sports car. When MG went modern in 1955 with their MG 'A' they also offered a twin cam variant, but it was not successful and the husky 1·6-litre ohv unit proved just as fast. In 1962 the MG 'A' became the 'B' with integral body/chassis construction, by which time a baby MG named the Midget, after its pre-war counterpart and based on the Austin-Healey Sprite, was continuing the tradition of a small, cheap sports car in the family.

On the Continent, the pattern of development which had commenced

A Rolls-Royce Carmargue; eight-cylinder, 6·75-litre, with a top speed of 119 mph (190 km/h) and everything else man could desire.

in the Thirties dictated that the European car was considerably advanced in specification when compared to its post-war British and American contemporaries. Independent all-round suspension was commonplace, and two-stroke engines and front-wheel drive were combined by firms like DKW and Saab.

Citroën of France fielded the sublime and the slightly ridiculous side by side with their advanced DS19 aerodynamic saloons and dropheads on the one hand and with the pre-war designed 2CV 'corrugated iron garden shed' on the other. The strange shape of the first DS19 shocked the public when first announced in 1955, but it did not date, and its unique self-levelling air suspension and power-assisted brakes, steering and gear-change made it as ahead of its time as had been its predecessor, the 'Traction Avant', in 1934. The 2CV combined an uncompromising ugliness with a simplicity of design and operation and a frugality which immediately endeared it to the French. It is still with us today in very much the same form in which it was introduced.

The best that Ford of Britain could offer in the early Fifties was the archaic Eight and Ten (in Anglia and Prefect guise) and the V-8 Pilot – the nearest that Dagenham ever got to Detroit 'Bulboidism'. These were

Left: The Triumph TR2 was introduced in 1953, running through a range of numbers to today's TR7, with its lively 2-litre, 16-valve, four-cylinder unit.

Below: A compact with good performance, the U.S. Ford mustang appeared in 1964. It sold half a million in 18 months. This is a late-Sixties model.

swept away and replaced by the stylish Consul, Zephyr and Zodiac in 1956 – some of the best-looking Fords ever built – but it was not until 1963 that Ford brought out a real winner in the Cortina. Combining good looks and performance with reliability and acceptability to tuning, it was attractive to both family and sporting motorist. 'Tweaked' by Colin Chapman, and in twin cam form, it was capable of 100 mph plus as the Lotus-Cortina.

Not all of Ford's new models were successful, however, and the Detroit parent dropped in 1958 what was perhaps the most classic automotive brick of all time with the Edsel. Named after Henry Ford's eldest son, and the result of extensive market research, this unfortunately-styled disaster took months to get into production, by which time the market gap at

Above: A 1980 Pontiac Firebird Trans-Am. With power at around 6½ litres, it has high performance but is a heavy gas-guzzler.

An Aston Martin DB3S of 1955, still in mint condition and with just 15,000 miles on the clock! It develops 230 bhp from 2·9 litres.

which it was aimed had closed. Ford persevered with it for three seasons and then wrote off umpteen million dollars to experience.

Chrysler never really regained their pre-war status in America (they had been the fastest growing newcomer during the Twenties) and they pitched from high-hipped ugliness to extravagant fins and other panel-beaters' nightmares in the Fifties and Sixties. In an effort to stave off disaster they widened their horizons and expanded heavily into Europe, taking over Simca of France (who had themselves absorbed Ford of France), and the ailing Rootes Group in Britain (which encompassed Hillman, Humber, Singer, Sunbeam-Talbot, Commer and Karrier).

Not all cars which sold well when imported into America were of sporting or high performance, and one of the most successful European small cars to break into the U.S. was the Volkswagen. Conceived in the Thirties by Dr. Ferdinand Porsche as Hitler's 'Strength through joy' car,

First seen in 1953, the fibreglass-bodied Chevrolet Corvette quickly became the sporting man's automobile, the only production sports car in the U.S.A.

in basic Kubelwagen and Schwimmwagen form it was extensively used by the German Forces during the war.

This odd little vehicle was evaluated by Humber in the aftermath of the war in 1945–6. On paper, its specification was not impressive. A beetle-shaped body on a backbone frame was propelled by a noisy, rear-mounted, air-cooled, horizontally-opposed engine which, in full song, sounded like a bag of old nails. Humber, with predictable British phlegm, found that the design held 'no merit', and plans to build it in Britain were dropped. Production was eventually commenced in 1945 in Germany under British control, and 1,785 cars delivered to the British Army. The factory reverted to civilian control in 1949 and thus Britain lost out on the greatest success story of the post-war era.

Progressively updated and increased in size from the original 1,131 cc of the early model to a hefty 1600 cc, the Beetle swept Europe and

Above: Replica cars are attracting a larger market than ever before. A fine example is this Panther Westwinds J72, built in traditional style by traditional methods, and somewhat reminiscent of the SS100 on page 59.

Left: Race-bred and roadworthy, the Ferrari 308 GTB, with its modest 2·9-litre engine, is capable of 250 km/h (155 mph).

America, and generally won the affection of the motoring public everywhere. Not only did it remain in production until the late Seventies, achieving the rare distinction of being the only single model to outstrip the Model T Ford's 15,000,000 total production, it also formed the basis of the outstandingly successful Porsche sports cars. The 911 series was progressively developed in six-cylinder form and the 907 2·2-litre prototypes were 1st and 2nd in the 1968 Sebring 12-Hour Race, gained a 2nd at Le Mans and won both the Monte Carlo and the Swedish rallies.

The Lotus Eclat 2+2 is a logical development of the Lotus line, which has become more de-luxe though no less sportive during recent years. Engine: four-cylinder 2-litre, with 160 bhp at 6200 rpm.

THE FUEL-SAVING SEVENTIES

By the late Seventies, Volkswagen were pinning their hopes at the popular end of the market on the Golf and the Polo. The Polo, like the Ford Fiesta and three or four almost indistinguishable contemporaries, reflects the current preoccupation with fuel conservation and general economy, but owes its transverse-engined front-wheel-drive to a much earlier pioneer.

Like the earlier Morris Minor, the Morris Mini-Minor and Austin

Seven of 1959 were both designed by Alec Issogonis and soon, simply dubbed the Mini, revolutionized small car design. Fitted with a 848-cc transverse engine driving the front wheels, and with the gearbox living in the sump, this compact little car boasted hydrolastic suspension, exceptional cornering ability and handling, and a susceptibility to tune which made it an immediate favourite with sporting motorists. In Cooper 'S' form, with a 1275-cc engine, it could sometimes even see off Jaguars in competition.

Jaguar, quite apart from their sporting successes with the XK120 and its derivatives the XK140 and XK150, entered motor racing officially in 1950, winning Le Mans no less than five times, in 1951, 1953, 1955, 1956 and 1957. In the last of these events, the unitary construction 'D' types finished in incredible fashion in 1st, 2nd, 3rd, 4th and 6th places. The

experience gained in competition resulted in a very successful line of saloon cars. The MkII was produced for 13 years and continued through the 420 and 'S' types, the 240, XJ6 and XJS to provide Jaguar's traditional formula of 'grace, space and pace'. It would certainly be correct to say that they never built a bad-looking car, and the 'E' type sports model caused a sensation when announced in 1961. With V-12 engine, the Series 3 'E' type took this ageless design well into the Seventies.

In the post-war period, take-overs were to be the order of the day in Britain. First to start the bidding were Standard, who purchased Triumph and developed their 1800 engine into the husky 2088-cc unit which powered both the Vanguard saloon and the solid and enduring little TR2 sports car. The David Brown tractor group absorbed body-

Below: This Aston Martin Lagonda represents the finest in British automotive electronic innovation and workmanship. Engine: 5·3-litre V8.

Below right: This 350SL Mercedes-Benz, renowned for its style and safety, was first seen in 1971. A sports-tourer two-seater convertible, its 3½-litre V8 unit gives it a top speed of 203 km/h (126 mph).

builders Tickford of Newport Pagnell, and Aston Martin and Lagonda, and transferred all operations there, giving W. O. Bentley's last design for Lagonda a new lease of life in both marques.

Leyland in turn took over Standard-Triumph, Jaguar bought Guy lorries and Daimler, Rover snapped up Alvis – keeping their military vehicle side going but phasing out their cars – and so it went on until, at last, the whole situation got completely out of hand. Then, under the direction of Donald Stokes – erstwhile super salesman of Leyland buses to China and Cuba – Leyland rapidly bought up everyone in sight and finished up with an enormously unwieldy empire which encompassed Rover, Riley, Austin, Morris, Wolseley, MG, Austin-Healey, Triumph, AEC, Albion, Guy, Jaguar, Daimler, et al.

Virtually the only companies to escape the take-over fever which pervaded the Sixties and Seventies were the very large, the very old, the very small and the exotic, and thus Rolls-Royce (despite the disastrous

bankruptcy of the parent aero-engine company in 1971) have remained healthily and individually Rolls-Royce, still able to command in the 1980s the respect which earned them the title of 'The Best Car in the World'. Post-war production centred initially upon the Wraith and Mk6 Bentley on updated versions of the old straight-six engine. It was not until 1959 that this configuration gave way to a 6·2-litre V-8 on the Cloud II and the S2 Bentley. Highly sophisticated transmission had, however, been standardized on the Cloud I and this feature was continued with the introduction of the completely new Silver Shadow in 1965.

There have been few true American sports cars. Ford made the Thunderbird of the Fifties and the semi GT Mustang in the Sixties, but both lost their initial sporting image after a few seasons as they grew heavier non-sports bodies, while Chevrolet's Corvette, born in 1953, retained the sporting persona for over a decade. Both Pontiac and Oldsmobile – particularly the latter's Tornado – have fielded models which are agile rather than sporting, but with the growth in popularity of saloon-car racing this absence of pure sports models has not been so much felt.

Of the Continentals the sleek Lamborghini, like Aston Martin, owes its existence to tractor manufacture. The Italian company has fielded an incredible assortment of post-war models ranging from a four overhead camshaft V-12 developing 360 bhp, to the Marzal with a 2-litre, six-cylinder engine and six headlamps!

Ferarri have continued to command world-wide respect in the competition world in a way in which no other Italian car, past or present, can hope to emulate. From their first Le Mans win in 1949, through the World Championships they gained for drivers of the calibre of Fangio,

The elegant Chrysler New Yorker 5th Avenue would grace any capital city. It is offered in four versions – a 2-door hardtop, a 2-door sedan, a 4-door sedan and a 4-door hardtop.

Hawthorn and Phil Hill, and the World Sports Car Championship wins of 1958, 1960 and 1961, they proved themselves again and again to be virtually invincible. While their Grand Prix fortunes have declined somewhat since the mid-Sixties, the early Seventies saw an amazing eleven consecutive wins in the Manufacturers' Sports Car Championship. Inevitably, Fiat now control the company, and the first fruit of the marriage – the Fiat Dino – boasted a Ferrari-designed engine.

Lancia, another old-established marque destined for Fiat control in 1969, have the enviable reputation of having never made a bad car. Their take-over was purely a matter of economics; in 1958 they had sold only 8794 cars to Fiat's 169,532. Happily, however, Lancia have retained for themselves a measure of independence, and the cars flying the Lancia flag represent the elite of the Fiat range. That this formula works was graphically demonstrated when, in December 1979, journalists voted the Lancia Delta – another transverse-engined small car – 'Car of the Year'.

The pooling of knowledge between rival companies and the production of components such as engines for common use is now increasingly popular. Both Peugeot and Volvo are involved in such schemes. To a lesser extent the theme is followed by the giants, with General Motors basing its small Chevrolets, Vauxhalls and Opels on a single master design, a distillation of technologies under one hood.

Oldest in the industry and still on top, Mercedes-Benz made a good recovery from the war years, and during the Fifties provided the car which won the Mille Miglia for Stirling Moss – the 8-cylinder, 3-litre 300 SLR – and indeed virtually every other major sports car event in 1955. The 300SL and its smaller cousin, the 190SL were both also highly successful as production models, and Mercedes have continued to

In the late Thirties American Bill Stout designed the bizarre Scarab, a vehicle with an interior like a living-room, in which the seats could be moved into various positions – even set up for card games. The streamlined body had no hood [bonnet] and a Ford V8 powerpack was housed at the back of the car. One of the few Scarabs actually built was used by General Eisenhower during his European campaign in the last war.

combine successfully sporting cars with high quality saloons and limousines – of which the 600 was the post-war equivalent of the enormous 'Grosser' beloved of Nazi leaders.

The years since the ending of the Second World War have been momentous and full of change. They have seen the ranks of the independents further decimated with only a few successful specialist newcomers, and the remaining makes brought together in massive groupings. The accent on safety has led most manufacturers away from open models so that now only the out-and-out sports car makers offer them. The world energy and fuel crisis, inflation, and the need for economy, has signalled the demise of the large and luxurious in favour of the efficient, compact, well-designed small car.

Now with two spectacular factors of the Seventies and Eighties – the risen sun of Japan, today in a strong position in the world's automobile markets – and the increasingly common automation of all facets of car-producing (such as Fiat's Strada which is produced almost untouched by human hand), the direction of car manufacturing is likely to be even more a matter for computer operators and promotion campaigns.

New techniques will engender new standards, and new restrictions on the use of fuel will call for new philosophies. Our new concepts of what constitutes adequate safety will also (perhaps even primarily) influence our conception of what constitutes a classic car. Certainly the accent is likely to be more on arriving at your destination in comparative safety than in the doubtful joys of travelling.

Just like it was when that first reliability trial was set up by *Le Petit Journal* in 1894.